Other Books by
William Murdock

Brisco: The Life and Times of National Collegiate
and World Heavyweight Wrestling Champion
Jack Brisco

Nikita: A Tale of the Ring and Redemption

Family Ties (contributor)

The Inklings at Christmastide

In the Final Analysis:
Mother Teresa's Enduring Message
to All Who Serve

As I See It:
Thoughts on Kindness in Action

FIND YOUR OWN
Calcutta

LIVING A LIFE OF SERVICE AND
MEANING IN A SELFISH WORLD

William Murdock

WESTBOW
PRESS®
A DIVISION OF THOMAS NELSON
& ZONDERVAN

Scripture quotations are taken from the Holy Bible, New International Version®, NIV®. Copyright © 1973, 1978, 1984, 2011 by Biblica, Inc.™ Used by permission of Zondervan. All rights reserved worldwide.

WestBow Press books may be ordered through booksellers or by contacting:

WestBow Press
A Division of Thomas Nelson & Zondervan
1663 Liberty Drive
Bloomington, IN 47403
www.westbowpress.com
1 (866) 928-1240

ISBN: 978-1-5127-9928-6 (sc)
ISBN: 978-1-5127-9926-2 (hc)
ISBN: 978-1-5127-9927-9 (e)

Library of Congress Control Number: 2017912726

Print information available on the last page.

WestBow Press rev. date: 08/21/2017

To all who have found their own Calcutta—in gratitude
of their dedicated, selfless service to others and to those
who are still seeking; it is closer than you may think.

CONTENTS

FOREWORD

One can change the world merely by being kind. There is no greater calling than to help those in need and less fortunate.

While those worthy attributes formed the foundation of a ministry that would elevate a diminutive Catholic nun to sainthood, they also apply to the author of this inspirational volume, a man who has dedicated his life to helping the disadvantaged.

In my four decades as a journalist, working with and writing about figures who have made significant contributions in various fields, rarely have I crossed paths with anyone the likes of William Murdock.

With a steadfast goal to reach out to those in despair, the poor and hungry of his community, Bill's vision grew from a simple yard sale more than twenty-five years ago to what has become an internationally recognized organization that now reaches more than 150,000 families each year. In partnership with Asheville businessman philanthropist Joe Eblen, Bill took a leap of faith and displayed how a little mustard seed could truly change the world.

As a friend and admirer, I've marveled at how this humble man has tirelessly helped transform an entire community. I once asked him why he chose to devote his life to such a cause. He replied simply, "The greatest thing anybody can do is to reach out to those less fortunate. We're all a day away, or a week away, from being in that position. There's no greater value to anyone's life."

His latest offering, *Find Your Own Calcutta*, came quite naturally, for it was the beautiful Christian example of Mother Teresa of Calcutta who provided much of the inspiration for Bill's work. One of the most beloved and important religious figures of our time, her life of service to the poorest of the poor—no matter what obstacles might occur—was a guiding principle for Bill's dedication to helping those less fortunate. Her mission was to serve and free the downtrodden from hunger, pain, and suffering.

Mother Teresa's example, says Bill, was no small influence on the philosophy of Eblen Charities. Like the woman who would be called "Saint of the Gutters," Bill Murdock has never allowed obstacles to get in the way.

Bill was in the beginning stages of setting up what would become known as Eblen Charities when he wrote to Mother Teresa and asked for guidance. She gave him that advice—and more—in a lengthy string of correspondence. That first letter many years ago would become the genesis of *Finding Your Own Calcutta*. It was a treatise on how all of us have the power to change the lives of those around us.

The book illustrates how Mother Teresa taught us by her example what it really means to "live" the gospel. From the slums of Calcutta to the whole world, she brought the message of selfless love for one's neighbor, regardless of race or ethnicity. She embraced society's outcasts when they had nowhere else to turn.

Her focus was on one person at a time, tending to each abandoned, hurting soul. "In this life," she said, "we cannot do great things. We can only do small things with great love."

She always said, "Never worry about numbers. Help one person at a time. And always start with the person nearest to you." Bill has been doing just that ever since.

While Mother Teresa is no longer with us, Bill reads her letters often, and a day rarely goes by that he does not think about her and her message. He keeps one of her letters in a frame that hangs next to his office door. It reads as follows: "God love you for all you are doing for the sick and poor. Do not worry if you cannot help in big ways. Never think a small action for someone in need is not much. For what Jesus sees is the love you put in to what you do. He will bless your little and multiply it like he did with the loaves."

Mirroring the absolute selflessness of a woman whose name is synonymous with compassion and caring, Bill has become a tireless benefactor of humanity. Eblen Charities has created programs to help feed the hungry, keep the lights on, and provide shelter and warmth, and much more under his direction. He continues to astonish and think big to spread hope one person at a time.

To Bill, it's not about Eblen or himself. It's all about the work. It's about the families they serve each and every day. Those are the real heroes—the folks who have the courage day after day to face difficult situations, every waking moment, wondering if they'll have enough medicine, if the lights are going to be turned off, or if their children will have enough food.

The Bill Murdocks of the world are there to serve as a safety net, to make sure they don't fall through the cracks. Bill Waddell, Eblen's esteemed community outreach director, calls his colleague "one in a million." "I think if you looked up the word servant in the dictionary, you'd probably see Bill Murdock," he jokes.

In 2014, Bill, along with Dr. John Maxwell, was awarded the Mother Teresa Prize for Peace and Leadership, an award that had previously been bestowed as the Mother Teresa Award to Pope John Paul II, Nelson Mandela, and the Dali Lama, among others.

Whether it be the inspirational weekly column he pens for Eblen Charities, the books he has authored on sports greats, such as collegiate and pro wrestling champion Jack Brisco, or volumes such as this that elevate the human spirit, Bill's words have the ability to touch the heart and soul, inspiring and challenging the way we think and live.

He is social enterprise's most intelligent writer and greatest asset.

Bill Murdock found his Calcutta. Won't you?

Mike Mooneyham
April 2017
New York Times best-selling author and columnist
The Post and Courier, Charleston, SC
2015 Pulitzer Prize winner

INTRODUCTION

I began writing this book on New Year's Day 2016. I am not sure that has any significance at all, but there is something about the dawning of a new year that brings a new glimmer of hope and another chance of getting things right.

So a new day and a new year is here, but so many have come and gone before, which causes me to wonder how much has really changed amidst countless resolutions to do better, live healthier, and be more understanding and kinder to each other.

Here in the United States we have just come through one of the most, tumultuous and divisive presidential elections in our history. By "coming through" I don't mean the vitriol on all sides has subsided since the last ballot was counted; on the contrary, it has just gotten worse.

It is not just here in America; it is evident around the globe. Terrorist attacks, bombings, and endless rhetoric laced with hatred and violence have sadly become commonplace. We shake our collective heads, mutter something about how terrible things have become, lose faith in those who promised to lead us, and watch woefully as the world goes on much the same.

I do believe, as I know so many do, that all is not lost—no matter how dark times may seem.

It is an indisputable truth that each year of our lives and each day that we have the privilege to live are full of moments that we will never again have in our grasp.

Each day allows us a fresh start and gives us a new hope that things will be brighter and that we have a renewed chance to not only make our lives better but help improve the lives of those around us.

What we have as each new year opens its days to us is a blank book containing 365 empty pages for us to create and write our stories. Each day we have a new, untouched page before us to inscribe the continuing narrative of our lives.

It doesn't matter what we have written before or if we haven't really written anything at all to this point. What truly matters is what we will write today and each day forward.

It is not what we inscribe taking pen to paper that is important; it is what we write with our lives, which is up to us and no one else. No matter what surrounds us, what it is that clamors for our attention and pulls us away from our heart of hearts, it is us and us alone who decide what we will write.

As we take each day—more important, as we take each moment of each day—let us promise ourselves to pause, even if only for an instant, and write not just about ourselves but about others.

It seems that we may hear the word "others" less and less in what has become an increasingly self-seeking world. With a "look at me" mind-set that manifests itself in what has become a "selfie" culture, the concept of others may have nothing more than a far distant ring to it.

It is far past the time when we dust off the idea that is as old as the scriptures themselves and make unconditional service to others new again.

As these new chapters of our lives open up to us, let us strive to let our pages be filled with the stories of those who have come into our lives. We will not just record them on paper but on the tablets of our hearts and very possibly the hearts of others.

Let us fill these new spotless pages with lives we have touched who are less fortunate, those who are hurting, those who are lonely, those who are hungry, those who are suffering, those who are tired, those who are afraid, and those who find hope and help just out of reach.

We don't have to look far for those in need; we just have to look. But looking and acknowledging they are there is not enough. Anyone— nearly everyone—does that.

It is easy to fall back into the mind-set of "I wish there was something I could do."

There is something you can do, something we all can do.

There always has been. And that is to be kind, share a kind word, help them through a difficult time by sharing what we have, and reaching out and putting those in need before our own interests.

Is there a way to truly change things? Yes.

Is it easy to do? Yes.

Can we start now? Yes.

Will it change things right away? No.

But it will change things and make a lasting change first in us, then in those around us, and then possibly further.

The question is where and how do we begin? Beginning is easy; the challenge comes in beginning it again each day.

In December 2015, Pope Francis declared 2016 as the Year of Mercy. So let us find the joy beginning in this Year of Mercy in rediscovering and rendering kindness and giving comfort to every man and woman of our time.

This isn't just a philosophy or empty rhetoric. It is a call to action, a call to all of us. This is the one thing that can draw us all together in a tumultuous world in the midst of troubled days.

It is a call to us to remember before we reach for hate that we remember the power of mercy.

The word *mercy* derives from the vulgar Latin (Latin traditionally spoken by the common Roman speakers of the time in contrast to classical Latin spoken and written by those who were educated) word *misericordia*, which meant "favor or pity." Our word mercy also comes from the Latin word *miseria*, which means "distressed or wretched."

So the meaning of mercy we have come to know is "giving pity or favor to the distressed or wretched," This is where the heart of service and a life of meaning lies. It lies in giving favor to those in times of need.

There is one common thread that I believe can transcend all of our differences. Not random acts of kindness but intentional and consistent acts of kindness.

So many are waiting for this—so many in our own communities, in our own cities, in our own country, and throughout the world.

Now is the time we have been looking for—a new chance to commit ourselves to others.

There is nothing on this earth stronger than kindness.

Let us show the world that we are strong.

We have a wonderful gift set before us in each new day that offers us an incredible opportunity to add a new volume of our lives' stories to embark.

This very well may be the best book we will ever write.

The idea of *Finding Your Own Calcutta* wasn't originally mine. It came from a letter that Mother Teresa had written nearly forty years ago. But in four simple words we can change our lives, our community, and the lives of those around us.

This book is written in the spirit of optimism and in the hope that the stories and thoughts that this volume contains will help to inspire those who may read it and to take heart, knowing that a life of meaning is so much closer than we might think.

This book contains stories of Mother Teresa's life and work as she reached out and selflessly served the "poorest of the poor" around the globe. It also includes stories of wonderful and amazing people who have found their own Calcutta and their own callings amidst the clamor of the world around them. These are stories of love and kindness in action.

Your own Calcutta awaits.

As Mother Teresa was known to say so very often,

"Let us begin …"

William Murdock
Arden, North Carolina
January 2017

Chapter 1

FIND YOUR OWN CALCUTTA

Find your own Calcutta.
—Mother Teresa of Calcutta

A few years ago I was invited by a small local group of aspiring young leaders to be part of a panel discussing needs and programs in our community in the areas of health and human services.

With more than fifty in attendance, we discussed what each panel member's organization provided to the community, gaps that we saw in existing services, progress we had seen in the past decade, future needs and concerns, and how we all were preparing to meet the challenges facing our community and organizations.

As interesting as the conversation was, it was the final question asked that brought why we were there into perspective.

The last question was simply, "What can we do? We would like to help and reach out, but we have full-time jobs and families. We can't spend the time and effort that you all do."

The answers that came from the panel were varied: find what you are passionate about, volunteer with an agency or group, get engaged with a cause that is near to your heart, and of course, donate to us and we will do the work.

As my turn came, I recalled a story that Mother Teresa had shared; I related it to those who were wishing to lead others there that morning.

Mother Teresa had received a letter from a young lady who had just graduated from college; the young lady had been following Mother Teresa's work for some time. She wanted to join Mother Teresa in Calcutta and dedicate her life to serving the poorest of the poor.

Mother Teresa received the letter and wrote back, and she said simply: "No."

She then went on to write:

> Stay where you are. Find your own Calcutta. Find the sick, the suffering, and the lonely right there where you are—in your own homes and in your own families, in your workplaces, and in your schools. You can find Calcutta all over the world, if you have the eyes to see. Everywhere, wherever you go, you find people who are unwanted, unloved, uncared for, just rejected by society—completely forgotten, completely left alone.

In sharing her story I was also reminded of another story Mother Teresa had shared that exemplified what she had written to this young lady.

"I had the most extraordinary experience once in Bombay. There was a big conference about hunger. I was supposed to go to that meeting and I lost the way. Suddenly I came to that place, and right in front of the door to where hundreds of people were talking about food and hunger, I found a dying man. I took him out, and I took him home. He died there. He died of hunger."

"And the people inside were talking about how in fifteen years we will have so much food, so much this, so much that, and that man died."

Calcutta was all around those who were there to change the world, and they literally had to step over this man who was dying of hunger.

Some time ago I was talking with someone I had met, and somewhere in our conversation the subject of serving those in need came up.

"I want to be famous and change the world," he told me.

"How?" I asked

"I don't know, but I want to be a superstar and change the world."

I asked him, "What about the people in our community in need of help?"

"What about them?" he asked.

He was ready for the world stage and all the accolades that he thought would follow, but his focus was far from sharp.

His focus was solely on himself. He saw helping others as the way to his gaining recognition and celebrity.

He was willing to make his mark on the world while totally missing the heart.

It amazes me that so many with kind and good hearts choose to ignore what is right outside their doors, instead choosing to set their sights on transforming the world.

They end up stepping over those in need, just as the attendees of the hunger conference did in Bombay to talk about ending world hunger.

In all my reading of history, I have found that the men and women who did indeed change the world never had that goal in mind at all.

Nor did they seek any recognition of their own. Mother Teresa, Martin Luther King Jr., Abraham Lincoln, and so many others never set out to change the world; they just set out and the world changed.

In these most trying and difficult times, we don't have to look any farther than our own backyards to find those who are in need and who are calling upon us, many times quietly, for our help and our kindness.

But the fact that they are there is not where the difficulty lies. We don't have to search to find those in need. We don't have to travel across the world to locate those who are suffering and lonely.

In fact, we don't have to drive across town to find them. They are all around us. They are not always part of what we see on television or what we have cemented in our minds as what those in need may look like. The men, women, and children in need are not always impoverished through a lack of material things, but so many of them are suffering with something all the more important—poverty of the heart.

The reality of it all is not that they are not there with us; the reality is that we don't hear them. We don't see them. Sometimes we turn our collective heads and pretend not to see, and at other times we are self-absorbed and tuned in to the distractions that surround us constantly.

Maybe, just maybe, if we take a moment and unplug, stop checking our smartphones every two minutes as if the world would stop turning without us, take the earbuds out of our ears and just listen for a moment, and put the tablet back on the shelf for a bit, we may actually see the world through our own two eyes instead of the digital eyes on which we have come to depend.

We can once again see the world as it really is, and we can begin to see the lives that encircle us. Are we that much in love with the sound of our own voices? Is it that we are so enamored with our own ideas, thoughts, and opinions that nothing else matters?

Is it that we are so captivated by our own intellects that we see ourselves as the center of the universe and believe that the world revolves only around us?

If that is the case, there is little wonder why we don't see or hear those who need our help. Perhaps if we stopped talking so much and stopped setting our sights on changing the world, we and the world would be better off.

As we all know, words only go so far. And if we, as Mother Teresa advised, find our own Calcutta and turn our good intentions into good works, changing the world will take care of itself.

Let us all remember that the pronouncement of good intentions is not where our work ends. It is where it begins.

Calcutta is waiting. But before we go any further, let us take a look at the woman who inspired and changed the world.

Let us begin…

Let Us Begin

- Don't set your sights on changing the world.
- Those in need of our help are all around us. We need not look beyond where we are.
- Poverty is not just a lack of material things; there is also poverty of the heart—a lack of love and kindness.
- It doesn't take much to turn good intentions into good works.
- We don't need to set out to change the world. We just need to set out and feed the hungry or visit a neighbor, and the world will change.

Chapter 2

SAINT OF THE GUTTERS

Do not wait for leaders; do it alone, person to person.
—Mother Teresa of Calcutta

In September 2016, the world stopped for a brief moment to once again remember Mother Teresa of Calcutta as Pope Francis canonized her, bestowing on her the sainthood of the Catholic Church. She became Saint Teresa of Calcutta.

Few since the annals of time began have lived a life of such selfless service to the world and to the poorest of the poor. In her simple act of answering what she said was "a call within a call," Mother (then Sister) Teresa left a life that she had already dedicated to serving others; she had been a Loreto sister and was pursuing a life of teaching and changing the world.

Although she touched the lives of thousands of children in the two decades she devoted to teaching, she couldn't escape the thoughts of the abject poverty that surrounded her and in which the children lived.

She left the comfort of the convent and the life she was living to commit herself to a deeper service; she chose to live among those she sought to serve.

Mother Teresa had a simple, quiet epiphany while she was on a trip and traveling by train from Darjeeling to Calcutta in 1948; she heard what she always referred to as a "the call within the call." And she knew without any doubt that she was to leave the comfort of her teaching and her convent and help the poor while living among them.

She would not serve them from afar; she would feed them, clothe them, and then retire where they were, not elsewhere. She would not just pray for them; she would live in their midst. She would be one of them. The world was changed with that one simple calling of the heart. Sister Teresa now had become Mother Teresa.

She started by picking up one woman who was dying—one woman, not dozens, not hundreds, and not thousands; just one. And in that compassion to that one forgotten woman, all of history stood still.

She was known as "the saint of the gutters," and if there ever was anyone who would have been picked to revolutionize the world, Agnes Bojaxhiu would not have been it.

Born in Skopje, Albania, on August 26, 1910, to Nikola and Dranafile Bojaxhiu, a prominent and prosperous family headed by her father, an entrepreneur, construction contractor, and broker of medication and other merchandise.

A devout family of the Catholic faith, both of Agnes's parents were deeply involved in their local parish and in the fight for Albanian independence.

Shortly after her eighth birthday, her father became ill and died suddenly, leaving Agnes alone with her mother and older brother and sister. But her father's death only brought the family closer, not only together but as they reached out to those around them who also found themselves in difficult times.

It was her mother's compassion and commitment to her neighbors that sparked her dedication to those less fortunate. Now having to struggle themselves, Agnes's mother opened their home continually to their community's poor and welcomed them all at her table.

She would often say to her daughter, "My child, never eat a single mouthful unless you are sharing it with others."

Agnes would frequently ask who were the people sharing a meal with them, and her mother would always respond, "Some of them are our relations, but all of them are our people."

Mother Teresa was always fascinated as a young girl by the stories told about the missionaries. She followed them closely, being able to locate any number of them on the map and was knowledgeable of what service and outreach was performed in each country.

Reared in the church and attending parochial schools, Mother Teresa first felt called to the "religious life" when she was twelve, and at the age of eighteen, she left her home in Albania to travel to join the Sisters of Loreto in Dublin, Ireland.

Founded in the seventeenth century to educate young girls, Mother Teresa began her service to the world with the Sisters of Loreto as a teacher. With a fierce determination and speaking a language that few of her fellow sisters could understand, during her novice year at the convent she was considered no more than "ordinary" and was viewed as "shy, quiet, and very small."

Even though she would answer another call and begin her own order, she always remained close to the Loreto sisters and always remembered them as where she began and the invaluable lessons and training she received there.

After a year in Ireland, Agnes was sent to Darjeeling, India, to finish her novitiate with the Sisters of Loreto. Two years later, she took her vows, choosing the name of Teresa, in honor of Saint Teresa of Avila and Saint Therese of Lisieux. Sister Teresa began her years of service to God teaching history and geography at Saint Mary's, a high school for girls in Calcutta.

Even though she touched the lives of countless children, she was constantly haunted by the wretched poverty that surrounded her and in which the children lived.

But it was in the fall of 1946 that Sister Teresa's world would change and with that, eventually, the entire world would change as well.

The then-thirty-six-year-old Sister Teresa was sent on her yearly retreat back to the convent at Darjeeling at the foot of the Himalaya Mountains, four hundred miles to the north of Calcutta.

She wrote about this in her journal: "It was a call within my vocation. It was a second calling. It was a vocation to give up even Loreto where I was very happy and go out in the streets to serve the poorest of the poor. It was in that train I heard the call to give up all and follow him into the slums—to serve Him in the poorest of the poor. I knew it was His will and that I had to follow Him. There was no doubt that it was to be His work."

In a simple, quiet epiphany, she heard God's call and knew, without any doubt, that she was to leave the comfort of her teaching and her convent and help the poor while living among them.

She began her outreach in Calcutta by teaching the children who lived in the streets. She would gather them in a small field or an empty alley, writing their lessons in the dirt with a stick.

She would not serve the poorest of the poor and those whose lives were discarded from afar. She would feed them, clothe them, and then retire where they were, not elsewhere. She traded the traditional habit of the Loreto sisters for a simple white-and-blue cotton sari, the same type of clothing worn by those she was to serve.

Mother Teresa never had big plans to change the world or to serve millions of people throughout the decades. Numbers were of no consequence to her.

She never saw the multitudes, even on the many occasions when there were multitudes pressing in around her. She saw only the one in front of her.

As she said many times, "One, one, one …"

This story has been told many times and has been shared in so many volumes, but it's one that shows the hallmark of not only her love and compassion but also how important one person was to her. Mother Teresa related this moving story:

> We have a place in Australia. (As you know, many of the Aborigines live there in very bad conditions.) When we went around in that place, we found an old man in a terrible condition. I went in there and tried to talk to him, and then I said to him, "Kindly allow me to clean your house, wash your clothes, and make your bed, and clean your bed," and so on.

He answered, "I'm all right like this. Let it be."

I said to him, "You will be still better if you allow me to do it."

He finally agreed. So I was able to clean his house (I call it a house, but it was actually not a house) and wash his clothes. I discovered that he had a lamp, a very beautiful lamp that was covered with dirt and dust. Only God knows how many years passed since he last lit it.

I said to him, "Do you light your lamp? Don't you ever use it?"

And he said, "For whom? Nobody comes here. I never see anybody. Nobody comes to me. I spend days without ever seeing a human face. I have no need to light the lamp. Who would I light it for?"

Then I asked him, "If the sisters come to you, will you light the lamp for them?"

He answered, "Yes, I'd do it."

From that day on the sisters committed themselves to visiting him every evening. The old man began to light the lamp for them and to keep it clean. He began to keep his house clean too. He lived for two more years.

Afterwards, he sent word to me through the sisters and said, "Tell my friend that the light she lit in my life continues to shine still."

That was such a small thing, but it was there in that darkness of loneliness a light was lit and continued to shine. A small action in deed, but it was one that had consequences that changed this lonely little man's heart and life forever.

How many lamps are waiting to be lit by our kindness? How many lonely and underappreciated people do we come in contact with every day, turning our heads, pretending not to see?

Just a moment of kindness—a smile, a touch of a hand—can light a lamp that would shine for all eternity. As we have seen in Mother Teresa's example, it doesn't take much. It was as simple as sharing her time.

Notice that she didn't convene a board or committee. She didn't say, "Let me pray about this, and I will see how God leads me." She knew God had led her to help for the very fact that he was standing there in front of her.

What more needed to be discussed or considered? We all would do well to follow Mother Teresa's example and not only see the need but to act without delay.

"Yesterday is gone; tomorrow has not yet come. We only have today. Let us begin," is Mother Teresa's encouraging principle to us all.

It is far past time that we find our own Calcutta.

Let us begin …

Let Us Begin

- Mother Teresa's life of service began as a teacher, not for what she was eventually known for, years later, around the world.
- There may be a "call within a call" in your life. Leave yourself open to what may be around you.
- We need not look for big things to accomplish. Remember Mother Teresa's example of seeing only the person in front of her—one, one, one.
- An act as simple as cleaning someone's house can light a lamp in someone's life that will continue to shine forever.
- Kindness does not work by committee. When you see someone in need, don't wait—act.

Chapter 3

WE ARE ALL ORDINARY MEN

All men are ordinary men; the extraordinary
men are the ones who know it.
—G. K. Chesterton

If that quote from author and apologist G. K. Chesterton's 1925 book
The Everlasting Man seems out of place in today's world, it may be
because it is.

A study by Media Dynamics reported that thirty years ago, an
average American was exposed to two thousand advertising messages a
day, compared to five thousand messages a day in 2014. That is thirty-
five thousand times a week that messages bombard us with what we
need to do to improve our lives, and that if we use a certain product,
wear a certain brand of clothes, or drive a certain type of car, we will
be set apart from the less intelligent, less worthy, or less special people
who surround us.

Image sells—and no advertisement that we see calls us to be
ordinary.

The last thing we want to be in this life is ordinary. Ordinary
is … well, just that—ordinary. Ordinary is for others who don't quite
measure up. Ordinary is for those who lack ambition. Ordinary is for
those who are not special. And after all, we are special, aren't we?

Well, at least a great number of us think we are.

So when did this all happen? When did kindness and humility take a backseat to arrogance and self-absorption? When did the Golden Rule begin to rust?

I don't think that anyone can pinpoint one place or time that our eyes and hearts turned inward, but there certainly has been a seismic shift toward a world that is more dominated by "selfies" than pictures of others.

It certainly is reminiscent of Carly Simon's 1972 hit song that glibly filled the airwaves with the question, "You're so vain; you probably think this song is about you … don't you, don't you?"

We all pretty much think it's about us—don't we, don't we? The salient truth is that it isn't, and it never was. We just think it is.

"All men are ordinary men; the extraordinary men are the ones who know it."

"God must have loved ordinary people because he made so many of us—and everyday ordinary people do extraordinary things."

These quotes could not have come from two more different people.

The first quote from G. K. Chesterton shatters the world of our self-perception, and the second quote comes from a man who had little in common with the British essayist, playwright, poet, artist, and theologian. What they had in common was the same Catholic faith and an understanding of where our true hearts should be.

The second quote comes from an amazing and courageous man whose leadership and example in the face of adversity resonates nearly a quarter century after his death from cancer.

The quote is from basketball coach and broadcaster Jim Valvano. "Jimmy V" led his North Carolina State Wolfpack to the NCAA Men's National Basketball Championship in 1983 against all odds, defeating the heavily favored University of Houston's Cougars.

There is more than a glimmer of hope to reset our hearts and sights to a life of service, regardless of the lives we have lived before.

But how far have we drifted from the simplicity, humbleness, and greatness of creating a life of reaching out to others?

Our own self-absorption and believing that we are the center of the universe has led us down a path that only leads us to focus on ourselves all the more and think about others less, if at all.

But maybe the truth and direction to the new path we are seeking doesn't lie in finding a new answer but in asking ourselves a different question.

How much would our world and the worlds of others change if we stopped asking the question, "What about me?" and asked, "How can I help?"

But first we have to set our compass away from pointing to us and set in service of others.

In his thought-provoking book *The Road to Character*, author David Brooks cited a Gallup Poll taken in 1950 that asked high school seniors if they thought themselves to be a person of importance. Only 12 percent answered, yes to that question.

More than a half a decade later, when asked the same question, 80 percent answered that they indeed thought of themselves as being important.

We have built a culture of celebrity that worships fame and where those we see on the screen or on the field, court, track, in the ring, or any of the countless venues that command our attention are higher in our regard than those who are far less known and touch the lives of those who are suffering in our community and around the world.

We have created an ethos of narcissism and a culture of celebrity. We have set ourselves up as stars and, in many cases, with a fan base of a very few and more times than not just ourselves.

A few years back I attended a multiyear reunion of my high school, T. C. Roberson. in a local restaurant owned by one of our classmates. As the evening went on, everyone was either catching up on the years that had gone by doing their utmost to try to impress those who were never impressed by them during their high school years or making sure that those who were impressed by them then still were.

After an hour or so, I found myself at a table of about fifteen or so classmates who were going around, answering questions posed by each member of the group in turn.

The questions were pretty typical, such as,

"Who was your favorite teacher?"

"What class did you like the most or the least?"

"Who did you have a secret crush on?"

But it was the final question and the answers that came in response that surprised me the most.

The question came from a lady who had graduated about six years after I did. The question was,

"What do you miss most about high school?"

Now, it had been more thirty years since most of them had roamed the halls of T. C. and for some of us longer, but for all of us, it was decades since any of us had been a student there.

Everyone answered the question almost the same. Or at least they all revolved around the same theme—popularity. They all seemed to miss being the center of attention of what was, as most of them declared the four years at Roberson High School, the absolute best years of their lives.

They had seen themselves as the ruling class of those four short years that for most of us were just filled with homework and heartbreak.

My answer about what I missed the most about high school was the meatloaf in the cafeteria (my grandmother was a wonderful cook but made terrible meatloaf, so I really enjoyed Mrs. Elingburg's in the cafeteria).

The last answer at the table, however, almost made my jaw drop. It came from an attractive lady who had graduated six or seven years after I left. She replied, "I miss being adored."

Everyone around the table nodded their heads almost in unison, accompanied with a sad and understanding smile.

"We all still adore you," one of our classmates said and all chimed in with their accolades as the former adored one smiled and, with tears in her eyes, replied, "Really?" Many left their seats and hugged her.

I never was in school with her, so I had no idea if she had been adored or not. It was obvious that she still had the need to be worshiped. The conversation continued as all talked about themselves, their accomplishments, and how important they all had become.

The focus hadn't lasted very long on the one whose lack of adoration brought her to tears. Everyone was back in his or her own world; the king and queen had returned to his or her own thrones.

What amazed me the most, I think, was that these were all nice people. Maybe it was just getting lost in the chemistry of the group, the nostalgia, and the fight for the spotlight. Maybe they didn't like the meatloaf.

But it did speak volumes about how we all are—or at least can be—if we are not careful.

When we treat people special, it is because we think that they are. We know that they are. If we see ourselves as the ones who are special above all else, we have very little, if any, capacity to see others in the same way.

We have no room for anyone else on the self-created throne we occupy. If we are special, then others can't be. There is only room at the top for one number one. It is either us or someone else.

No man can serve two masters. We can't serve others and ourselves. We have to make a choice. But as Bob Dylan wrote, "You gotta serve somebody."

There is also something else we should be aware of, and it is the simple fact that if we treat someone as a king or queen long enough, eventually that person will start to act that way.

Even if we are the only ones who see ourselves as royalty, we will begin to treat ourselves that way and expect others to do so as well.

It seems as if we have become a society of millions of self-serving kingdoms led by a single monarch—us—and in doing so, we find ourselves ruling over a kingdom populated by a single inhabitant—us again.

David Brooks went on to cite some other interesting facts about how so many see themselves.

Psychologists use an assessment called the narcissism test. The test is given by reading certain statements and inquiring whether or not the particular statements relate to the person.

The statements ranged from "I think I am a special person" and "I wish somebody would someday write my biography" to "I like to be the center of attention" and "I am more capable than other people."

If there has been any reservation about the fact that we are accelerating toward the self-seeking world that revolves only around us and the existence that we have created, it is interesting to know the trends of the narcissism test the past few years.

The median score has risen almost 95 percent during the past two decades, with the largest increase being in the area of thinking that "I am an extraordinary person." Self-esteem and narcissism run amok.

The desire for fame also has risen exponentially. More than half of the young people surveyed less than ten years ago stated that being famous was at the top or near the top of their goals. In the same survey taken in 1976, gaining fame ranked much lower, coming in fifteenth out of sixteen listed goals.

With that, it should be no surprise that in a 2015 poll of the most admired people in the world, conducted by the online Business Insider, business mogul Bill Gates and actor Jackie Chan ranked higher than Pope Francis and the Dali Lama, while soccer star David Beckham and actor George Clooney ranked higher than the Reverend Billy Graham.

If all of that hasn't at least started you thinking that maybe we are indeed entrenched in a selfish world, we can probably at least agree that we live in a "selfie" world.

By now I think everyone who is even somewhat familiar with technology knows what a selfie is. If you don't, you don't have to look any further than the *Merriam-Webster Dictionary*.

Its definition is "selfie: noun / self-ie—an image of oneself taken by oneself using a digital camera, especially for posting on social networks."

From the first known use in 2002, the selfie has become a part of our daily routine that has added to the "Hey, look at me" part of our culture. It is now reported that more than a million selfies are taken each day, and a study by the *Daily Mail* in the UK estimates more than seventeen million are taken and uploaded weekly and posted on Facebook, Instagram, Twitter, LinkedIn, and other social media sites.

This is all for the purpose of showing the world where we are and how important we are to ourselves—and should be to everyone else.

A recent study estimated that those born into the millennial generation—those born between the years 1980 and 2000—will take nearly twenty-six thousand selfies in their lifetimes.

It is not just the millennials who are taking pictures of themselves. The same study in the United Kingdom cited that more fifty-five-year-olds are taking selfies than the eighteen- to twenty-four-year-olds.

And when we are not doing that, we are checking our smartphones up to one billion times a day, worldwide.

All this is not to say these habits that have become so ingrained in us are wrong or evil in themselves, but it certainly has taken over or at least taken precedence of our individual and collective thoughts.

And it can only guide us in one direction—one of nothing but self-centeredness, which leads us to a most dangerous place, and that is a place of arrogance. It is that arrogance that convinces us that we are far better than everyone else. This pride blinds us to the needs of others because to us they just don't matter.

Again, we can't look inwardly and outwardly at the same time. As we only look inward, we magnify to ourselves who we are and diminish everyone else. This may not happen consciously, but it happens all the same.

No one whose life is filled with hubris, even those who are "humble braggarts"—those who feign humility as they boast of their achievements and recognition—ever truly win.

It is nothing but an empty hole that, no matter how hard we try, will never be filled. It is a ravenous hunger that once it starts only continues to grow and can never be satisfied.

It keeps us running toward a goal that will always be just out of reach and in the end will obtain hollow achievements at best. As the scripture says, "Pride comes before destruction and a haughty spirit before a fall" (Proverbs 16:18).

With all of this surrounding us, how do we change direction, swim against this raging tide of selfishness, and realize that we are all alike and in the same boat?

When will we be able to look up from our smartphones and tablets and see those who are in need of a smile, a kind word, or a compassionate open heart?

I don't believe those who have these things to give ever lost them. We just need to remember where to find them again.

So the question remains: where do we find this caring heart and take the first steps to a life of service?

It is far closer that we might think, and it starts with a concept that at times seems almost lost in our "selfie age": the simple concept of humility.

For those of us who may have lost sight of what humility is, author, educator, and theologian C. S. Lewis probably gave one of the best definitions of what it really is when he wrote, "True humility is not thinking less of yourself; it is thinking of yourself less."

If there is a shining example and personification of a life of humbleness, it is Mother Teresa. To her, there was a singular and unique strength that comes with humility.

"If you are humble nothing will touch you, neither praise nor disgrace because you know who you are," Mother Teresa would tell us. "If you are blamed you will not be discouraged. If they call you a saint, you will not put yourself on a pedestal."

Armed with the strength and freedom that humility gives, Mother Teresa quietly led what would be seen a decade later as a revolution that changed the hearts and lives of millions.

A well-known story of Mother Teresa happened some forty years ago in Calcutta.

Late one evening her sisters came to her, concerned that there was no bread for the next day for them to feed the hundreds who would be at their door in a few short hours. Mother Teresa, undaunted by the news, told her sisters, "Earnestly pray and go to bed; tomorrow, if need be, we will beg on the streets to feed the poor."

Very early the next morning, some schools in the area were closed unexpectedly, and truckloads of bread that were designated for the schools went to the Missionaries of Charity.

I have known of this story for some time, but just recently was I made aware of the second part of the story. I knew well about the lack of bread, and its unexpected delivery, with no explanation of why the schools were suddenly closed.

But what I didn't know was that Mother Teresa had told them if the bread did not come, they would go out on the streets and beg for the poor themselves.

What struck me in hearing this story again after so many years was not the arrival of the bread, which many, including me, would see as a miracle, but the fact that Mother Teresa would not send the poor away hungry to beg on their own.

She and her sisters would beg on their behalf. Mother Teresa was not going to convene a task force on hunger, send her staff, or see what she could do.

This tiny Albanian nun, who had been visited by kings, queens, princes, princesses, and presidents and who had won the Nobel Peace Prize, was willing and planning to go out and beg for food for those she believed that God had entrusted in her care.

No committees, no speeches, no assessment of the need; she knew people were hungry and that was all that mattered.

Mother Teresa had been known to say, "Don't wait for leaders. Do it yourself, person to person." While others may have met over breakfast or lunch to discuss the hunger of those outside their doors, Mother Teresa and her sisters were prepared to do what was necessary to feed those who were hungry that morning.

There is no better example of service to all of us who want to reach those who are less fortunate, and the salient question is how far are we willing to go to help someone whom we know is in need of our help?

So the questions are: Are we willing to put aside our self-importance and humble ourselves enough to do what Mother Teresa did so often? Are we willing to actually put ourselves as she did and humbly work on the behalf of those suffering? Are we prepared to do so without the first thought of how it would look and what people would think?

She was not worrying about the whispers and gossip of false friends and true enemies. Her concerns were for those suffering and for them alone.

If Chesterton had known Mother Teresa, would he have thought of her as ordinary? Without a doubt, yes. But I can only imagine how extraordinary he would have seen that her work was.

Even with all the accolades, Mother Teresa saw herself as only ordinary, such that she would frequently say that she was a "pencil in God's hand and he writes what he wants."

"All men are ordinary men; the extraordinary men are the ones who know it."

Let us begin…

Let Us Begin

- The world around us calls us to be anything but ordinary, and as Chesterton pointed out, only the extraordinary know how ordinary we really are.
- In the unending clamor with which we are surrounded, telling us how important we are, it is easy to have our heads turned and lead us to believe we are more special than others.
- The more we look inward, the less time and desire we have to see the world around us.
- We would all do well to follow Mother Teresa's example and be willing to go out on behalf of those in need and ask for help.
- We must all decide whether we will set aside our own self-importance, turn our sights around, stop looking at ourselves, and look at those around us.

Chapter 4

WHY WE ARE HERE

The purpose of life is not to be happy. It is to be useful,
to be honorable, to be compassionate, to have it make
some difference that you have lived and lived well.
—Ralph Waldo Emerson

If our purpose in life is just to be happy and to serve ourselves, then we have no purpose. Since the beginning of time, man has searched for true meaning caused by a deep longing that there has to be something more than just meets the temporal eye.

If our lives are solely based on our seeking our own happiness, we will only find the world to be an empty and lonely place. And that is because we are trying to find purpose where purpose doesn't exist. We are only trying to catch the wind.

One night I was having dinner with an old friend, and we began talking about what was going on in our lives, and he said that he realized that all he wanted out of life was to be happy.

Now, my friend had a nice family and had done well professionally. He had a nice home and everything you could imagine. But all he wanted was to be happy.

Certainly there is nothing at all wrong with wanting to be happy. After all, who wants to miserable? But he told me that being happy would be his goal from now on. His reason for living was his own happiness.

What struck me from that comment was that it was something I would expect to hear from a teenager, not from a good man who had accomplished so much.

What was so heartrending to me was that with so much going for him, the happiness he sought was always out of reach because he never realized that finding happiness in just being happy never comes.

The door he was trying so desperately to get through, sadly, was locked from the inside. The happiness he was trying to achieve wasn't out of reach; it was there for him, but he had to look outside of himself instead of within.

It wasn't long after that I came across the quote at the beginning of this chapter. Rereading this a number of times, I could see why my friend and so many others, including me at times, had never found the happiness we all sought.

Ralph Waldo Emerson grew up in the mid-nineteenth century and gained fame as an author, lecturer, essayist, educator, and poet. His thoughts and writings centered on self-reliance and individualism, and, whether or not one may agree or disagree, at the center of his thoughts lies an amazing truth: "The purpose of life is not to be happy. It is to be useful, to be honorable, to be compassionate."

Ironically, if we are useful to others, honorable, and compassionate to those in need, it is then we find the happiness we seek.

So now that we have some idea of where we are and who we have become as a people, how do we turn things around? How do we muster the love and compassion we need to put others first and ourselves last? Where and when do we begin?

Where we begin is here.

When we begin is now.

I believe we really don't have to look very far to find what we need to begin or to continue our lives that are committed to those in need. If we search the depths of our hearts, we may very well find that all that we need is much closer than we think.

We all have our beginnings with the direction in our lives, and it is my hope that somewhere, all of us had at least an inkling of what a life that focuses on others is like.

Fortunately this direction came to me early in my life. I wish that I could say that I never veered from what I was taught and the tremendous example I had afforded to me, but that would be far from the truth.

Regrettably I have done more than my share of going my own way and thinking only of myself more often and for a much longer period of time than I would like to recall. And sadly, I find myself still doing that from time to time, no matter how hard I try not to.

But I continue to do better and think of myself less and others more. I will continue to raise my sights. We must all continue to raise our sights.

My early education in the art of thinking of others came by way of example more than conversation or lectures.

It came from my grandparents.

My grandfather, Joseph Goetz, was born in Green Bay, Wisconsin, in 1911, and my grandmother, Mildred Paap, a year later in Milwaukee. Grandpa's family moved to Milwaukee when he was about ten years old, where he met Grandma and married in 1934 in Wauwatosa at Saint Bernard's Church.

Two years later my mother was born. My grandparents named her Marilyn Ann for no other reason that I know of other than they liked the name. She was their only child, and her days ended far too soon.

She died when she was twenty-two from complications from a miscarriage shortly before my second birthday. When she died my grandparents took me in and gave me a home.

Both my grandparents were kind and generous; as I remember, their door was always open to everyone they met, as it had been to me. They shared their time and money with those in need and would never say a word.

My grandfather was a man of deep faith and conviction. He never talked much about it, but there was never any doubt what he believed or what made him the man he was.

My earliest memories of Grandpa's kindness came every Sunday when he would give me an extra dime or quarter and walk with me to the "poor box" by the door of the same church in which he and my grandmother and my parents were married.

He would lift me up to drop the coins in the box and remind me how important it was to always remember to reach out to those who might be less fortunate.

He told me that it didn't matter how much I gave, and that even if I couldn't give a lot, what was important was that I always remembered to share what I had with those in need.

He told me that God didn't look at the amount but at our hearts, and that we gave not from any extra that we might have but from what we might have given up to help others.

I remember one day asking, "Grandpa, why are we here?"

He answered simply, "To help others."

I am not sure my eight-year-old mind could quite fathom his answer, but I do remember asking him, "Then what are others here for?"

"So we can help them," Grandpa answered.

Greek author and philosopher Plato has been attributed to have said, "Be kind, for everyone you meet is fighting a hard battle."

We are or have been all bound by one thing or another in our lives.

We pretend that we aren't or haven't, but we all have.

We pretend that we can make it solely on our own. We think that needing help shows a degree of weakness.

But I think it is just the opposite.

Some time ago I came upon this story that exemplifies that.

A female humpback whale had become entangled in a massive web of crab traps and lines.

She was weighed down by hundreds of pounds of traps and had hundreds of yards of rope wrapped around her body and her tail, as well as a line tugging in her mouth, all of which caused her to struggle to stay afloat.

A fisherman just east of the Golden Gate Bridge spotted her and immediately radioed for help.

Quickly the rescue team arrived and determined that the only way to save her was to dive in and untangle her.

This was, at best, a very dangerous plan, as one blow from her tail could kill any of those who were attempting to rescue her. They worked for hours, cutting the lines and traps that entangled her, and eventually set her free.

Then a most miraculous thing happened. The divers witnessed her swimming in circles, seemingly joyful in her regained freedom.

She then came back to each and every diver, one at a time, nudged them, and pushed gently, thanking them.

The diver who cut the rope out of her mouth says her eye was following him the whole time.

He remarked that he would never be the same again.

In freeing her, he and all those who worked tirelessly to unbind her were themselves set free as well.

A life of service to others sets everyone free.

Whether we are freeing a whale or calling to check on a neighbor or holding a door open for someone, it is all the same. An act of kindness has eternal implications that grow exponentially with every benevolent action.

Strength and deliverance can come through the hands of others as much as they do from our own. As mighty as the whale was, it couldn't find the way to set itself free. It needed others. But if our hands are too busy garnering things for ourselves, we can't have the room we need to use them to help others.

The things that bind us may not be as apparent as the traps and lines that held the majestic whale captive, but just because they may be invisible to the eye does not make them any less real or difficult. But we are placed here to help. That is what my grandpa was teaching me all along.

I am pretty sure that my grandfather never read Plato. But then again, I guess that he didn't have to after all.

It is my hope that we all may be so fortunate in our lives to be surrounded by people who will help us get untangled from the things that are binding us and that we all are willing to help untangle those who come into our lives for no reason other than we are all the same and that we are able to help.

Mother Teresa knew this best of all. She saw firsthand for decades the kindness that she inspired that came from those who at times were hurting the most.

One day a gentleman came to Mother Teresa and told her about a family he knew that was in need. "Mother," he said, "there is a Hindu family that has eight children, and they have not eaten in a long time. Please do something for them."

Mother Teresa immediately gathered some rice and took it to them. When she arrived at the family's home she could easily see the devastation that the hunger had brought upon them.

As she talked with the mother and her children, she could see hunger in their eyes. Their eyes shone with hunger as they gratefully accepted the rice. But as she handed the rice to the mother, she witnessed an amazing thing.

The mother took the rice and began to divide it in two and then went out, carrying half of the rice with her. When she came back, Mother Teresa asked her where she had gone with the rice.

She told Mother Teresa simply, "They are hungry too." She continued by telling her that she had neighbors whom she knew had not had anything to eat for quite some time as well. Because she knew, she shared what she and her children had been given.

The same lesson that my grandfather worked so hard to teach me was the same one that Mother Teresa and this mother, who had been facing hunger, knew so well.

True love, as Mother Teresa taught, involves sacrifice.

Giving from our surplus may help those to whom we are giving, but it robs us of the true heart of what true giving is about.

This mother was willing to share the food that was brought to her with a family that faced the same plight—not only sharing the rice with a neighboring family but with a Muslim family. Hindus and Muslims in India did not have anything to do with each other. But love, compassion, and shared hunger trumped religious fervor.

The mother and her children understood. They understood the pain of hunger, loneliness, and despair. That is why she did not hesitate for an instant to share the food she and her children so desperately needed.

We don't have to travel to India to find those who are hungry, lonely, and in need of help.

But again, we have to do more than think about ourselves and take the time to look beyond the surface and reach out to those who are hurting—hurting not just for food or other temporal needs but hurting for kindness, a smile, and for someone to let them know that their lives matter; someone to let them know that they are not alone.

If that wonderful mother would take half of the precious food that Mother Teresa gave her and her children and share it with a family that socially she was not even to acknowledge, what is stopping us from setting ourselves aside for a while to touch someone's life with kindness and compassion?

The only thing holding us back is our own selfishness. We are not trying to change the world here; we are just trying to help touch the hearts of those in need and, in the process, change ours as well.

Let us begin …

Let Us Begin

- The purpose of life is to be useful and compassionate to others, not to focus on our own happiness.
- We don't have to wait to begin or look to someone else to lead us. As Mother Teresa said, "Do it yourself, person to person."
- Remember the true heart of giving is in our sacrifice, not in giving from abundance.
- We can only raise our sights for others by lowering our sights from ourselves.
- Be kind, for everyone is fighting some kind of battle.

Chapter 5

CREATING A LIFE OF SERVICE

Service to others is the rent you pay for your room here on earth.
—Muhammad Ali

That quote has been one of my favorites and one that has remained in my thoughts almost daily since I ran across it a dozen or so years ago. When I first read it, I was more than a bit surprised at who first spoke these words. It wasn't Mother Teresa, Dr. Martin Luther King, or Mahatma Gandhi. Those simple but powerful words came from Muhammad Ali.

Yes, that Muhammad Ali—the American prize fighter, Olympic champion, activist, author, philanthropist, Presidential Medal of Freedom recipient, Hall of Fame inductee, and three-time heavyweight champion of the world who passed away on June 4, 2016, at the age of seventy-four.

But the question still remains: how do we begin to create a life of service that will give our lives meaning and will touch the lives of those in need but will transform our lives as well?

The first step is to turn our good thoughts and intentions into actions. The decision to reach out to those in need or the declaration of living a life of service is not where our new life ends but only where it begins.

But we don't need to keep thinking about it. No more meetings and no more talking about what we want to do.

Along the same vein of Muhammad Ali, the legendary Chinese American martial artist, actor, philosopher, author, entrepreneur, filmmaker, and founder of jeet kune do, Bruce Lee, once noted, "If you spend too much time thinking about a thing, you'll never get it done."

So why are we waiting to create a life of service? The longer we think about helping others and beginning or growing in our life of service, there is a good chance that we may never start at all. And every day we delay we are missing so many wonderful opportunities to make a difference in others' lives and in our own.

The longer we wait, the longer others may suffer or be lonely. The longer we wait, the longer we postpone the joy that can come only by serving others and bringing joy to their lives.

This is not that we are thinking of ourselves less but are thinking of others more.

I believe that kindness begets kindness. By this I mean the kinder we are and the more purposeful and conscious acts of thoughtfulness we do, the more and more we may do them unconsciously, and we may be surprised that in no time they become part of who we are.

I found a great example of this one morning in our staff meeting. We were finishing up, and, as usual, I was reading to my coworkers the comments that clients had written on the bottom of their client survey forms. We ask every client to fill out a survey and write any comments they would like to make so we can see how we are doing with our client service.

In reading some of the comments, this particular group of surveys mentioned how nicely they had been treated while at Eblen Charities. The conversation continued as we discussed the importance, above everything else, to treat everyone with great consideration and courtesy.

One coworker smiled and said, "You know, we keep talking about how we all treat our clients here in the office, but I find myself doing the same thing out of the office too."

"How's that?" I asked.

"Well, for one thing," she answered, "I keep letting people in front of me in the checkout line at Ingle's when I am grocery shopping. And I don't even know them."

As with a great many groups, we at Eblen Charities not only talk about treating everyone with the highest esteem, but we also make sure that we treat everyone with whom we come into contact with the utmost respect.

All that starts with something very simple. It is as powerful as it is simple. It starts with a smile. It starts with a kind word and taking a moment to greet and talk to those we see.

We make it a point to warmly greet everyone who comes into Eblen's Waddell Client Service Center. We address them by Mr., Mrs., or Ms., unless they request we call them by their first names.

We offer coffee, water, and doughnuts every morning. On days that we have a great number of clients and they may have to wait through lunch, we bring lunch in for all our clients, staff, and volunteers, thanks to Joe Brumit of Arby's and Dini Pickering of the Biltmore Company.

Even with these things there is nothing that takes the place of the kindness that our families see in our smiles, that they see in our eyes, or that they see in our faces and hear in our voices.

Of the hundreds of client surveys we receive each week, two stick in my mind most of all. One is an answer a client gave for the question, "Intake worker seen?" She responded, "The nice one." That one would be difficult to track down; it could have been any one of our staff.

The second one that comes to mind was a comment that one gentleman made at the bottom of the survey sheet. He wrote, "I wasn't expecting anyone to help me today. Thank you so much for your kindness. This has been a good day."

I can't imagine a greater comment or compliment for anyone to have said—"This has been a good day," especially from someone I am sure doesn't experience many good days.

It is so easy to go through the motions of helping those less fortunate and totally miss the heart of what we are trying to do. The only way to truly touch the hearts of those we seek to serve cannot be just by providing temporal things, as important as they are.

The attitude we possess in helping those in need is where our heart of hearts lies. If we reach out our hands to those who are struggling with an attitude of superiority, arrogance, and the thought that we are better than they are, and we think, *Aren't we good people to lower ourselves to give from our excess to those who find their lives out of their control?*, we lose everything that we are meant to gain by giving.

Those we help may receive the food, housing, or heating assistance they need, but they also receive what they need the most and deserve to have more than anyone. And that is our respect and our kindness.

If we don't serve in that manner, those we help may miss the most important part of our giving—the heart of our kindness. And that is the same kindness that God has shown to us and calls us to share with all who come into our lives.

Recently we were part of a group that worked together to provide free dental care to our community for two days. We had been part of this effort before, as one of our board members, Dr. Jack Teague, brought this wonderful project to Asheville. For three years we held the outreach at our local community college, Asheville-Buncombe Technical Community College, where, for more than two days, we saw nearly eight hundred folks in need of dental care that they may have not been able to afford for years.

Hundreds lined up the day before we were to open the doors to the clients, and the group that ran this amazing program told our local group horror stories of fights in line, destroying restrooms, and leaving the site in shambles.

One comment that was made about those we were to serve surprised me. One of the members of the group said, "They will destroy everything—that is the type of people they are and that is why they are in the situation they are in and have to come here for free dental care."

I couldn't believe what I was hearing. I told him that those we would see in those two days were wonderful and courageous people. I told him that these were good people, and if we treated them as such we would have no problem.

And we had no problem. We welcomed everyone in line, thanked them for being there and for their patience, and said how appreciative we were of A-B Tech, who helped make the event possible.

We also asked them to help us pick up and keep the area clean, and if they saw any problem in the restrooms or anywhere else to please let one of the volunteers know. By the end of the two-day event, there was not one fight and not one restroom destroyed or even left untidy.

We treated those who came to us with respect, and they treated us the same way.

A few years later we were once again working with this group and with a tremendous and giving church in our community. As we were walking through Biltmore Church to see how we were to set it up, again we were told the type of clients to expect.

The folks at the church were told to make sure that they had plenty of port-a-johns on site and to make sure that they did not let the clients use the restrooms, as they would destroy them, as they had little if any regard for others' property.

Members of our local group reminded this young man who had such a dim view of those we were trying to reach that we didn't have any trouble at A-B Tech for the three years we had held it there.

As we finished our walk-through, I spoke with Kelvin Mosley, one of the ministers at Biltmore Church, who oversaw their outreach. I told him that these were indeed good folks, but I didn't have to say much.

"I know these are good people. How could we say that we will help fix their teeth but they can't use our restrooms?"

Kelvin added, "That would be a terrible insult to those who are going to be on our campus."

Kelvin didn't have to give a moment's thought to show his kindness and the heart of Biltmore Church, and those who came that weekend received much more than the dental care they sought. Their hearts as well as their church was open to all, thanks to Kelvin, the great leadership of Pastor Bruce Frank, and an amazing staff and members.

To build a life of service, again we have to stop looking inward, or the only persons we will ever serve will be ourselves.

How can we know the world around us, with all of its wonders and opportunities to help others and truly change it, if we look for the answers only within ourselves?

So much of the advice we have been fed by the shovelful has been directed with ourselves being the center of the universe.

How many parents, teachers, commencement speakers, and others tell the legions of young people to find what they want to get from life and go after it? You deserve it, you are special, and because of that, you deserve to be happy, above all.

If we ask ourselves a different type of question, we will more than likely come up with a different answer. Instead of asking, "What is it that I want out of life?", we should ask, "What does life want out of me?"

What if we ask, "What talents have I been given? What is it that my community, my state, my country, and the world at large need that I can do?"

The answer certainly would be different than if we continue to ask, "What do I want?" But that answer will be the one that sets us on the path to genuine service to others, and with that we may very well find the happiness for which we all long.

My grandfather used to tell me, "Find a need and fill it."

"How?" I would ask.

"Pray for your vocation, and you will find what you are supposed to do, and when you do, you will find out who you are."

What I believe that Grandpa was trying to tell me was that instead of looking to lead our lives, we should look to where our lives lead us. He was guiding me to realize that the most important answers in life are not found within us but on what we encounter on the outside world around us.

As Mother Teresa pointed out, Calcutta is all around us. We have already found it, or it has found us. So we have to figure out what it is we can do to make things better for those that we have found in our own Calcutta.

Do not doubt for a moment that there is a reason we are placed where we are. The meaning of life is right in front of us.

But once again, we simply have to start.

In the first letter that Mother Teresa sent me, she wrote:

Dear William:

God love you for all you are doing for the sick poor. Do not worry if you cannot help in big ways. Never think a small action done for someone in need is not much. For what Jesus sees is the love you put into what you do. He will bless your little and multiply it like he did with the loaves.

God bless you,
Mother Teresa, MC

Isn't it amazing how the most important messages come in so few but such powerful words?

"Do not worry if you cannot help in big ways. Never think a small action done for someone in need is not much …"

As she wrote to me later: "Do not try to change the world in one go." We have to begin with what we have and where we are.

Mother Teresa showed throughout her life and ministry that no job, no matter what it may have been, was too insignificant. In fact, it is not the task at hand that may be important; it's the heart and willingness to do what is before us.

It is just as much, if not more, about the attitude we have in doing it. It is about what spirit we possess and the joy we find in having the opportunity to serve even in the smallest way.

Small actions can often have large and everlasting results. Think about the last time someone showed kindness to you. How did you feel after someone called to wish you a happy birthday or sent you a note to see how you were feeling after they heard you might be sick?

These may not be big things in the entire scheme of the universe, but they meant something to you. Just the fact that someone else was thinking about you and took the time to acknowledge that you were important to him or her had to make you smile and remember that action.

Mother Teresa also knew that no matter how small any act of service was, it was vital to a much larger mission.

It is not only what we do but how we do it—that is every bit as important.

Mother Teresa many times reminded us, "We are not called to be successful; we are called to be faithful."

The faithfulness and joy with which we perform the service to others helps build the spirit we need to continue on to the next opportunity and turn us into who are meant to be.

Our acts of kindness are the same. A small act is part of a much bigger picture in our lives and in everyone we encounter.

The world around us and the needs that we see, even in our own communities, can be daunting, at best. It may be difficult to see what the bigger picture actually is and how our small acts can make any difference at all.

We all must keep in mind that it is in the simple act of starting that those worlds and lives can be changed.

Building everything takes time, patience, effort, and energy.

It may take years to build. In an age of instant everything, so many of us who wish to serve rarely are willing to take time to build.

We want to help as many people in need as possible and want to do it now, so it is easy to lose sight of why we want to help. Numbers get to be more important than why we want to serve others in the first place.

It is well known that Mother Teresa's work started modestly. Not long after she arrived in Calcutta, she came upon a woman dying in the gutter. The woman was covered with insects, and rats were ripping away at her flesh; their hunger and viciousness would not let them wait until death came.

Passersby barely noticed. This was not something of their concern. Scenes such as this were commonplace, so no notice was given to this woman whose life was fading away in this sewer. They rushed by, not even giving a fleeting look, any more than they would to garbage discarded in the street.

Moreover there were far too many people like this in Calcutta for anyone to make a difference by getting their hands sullied with this one old woman.

But the newly arrived Sister Teresa had no doubt about what she had to do, although she had no idea just how to do it.

With no organization, staff, volunteers, or money and with no vision of anything more than helping this one woman, she picked up the woman and carried her to a local hospital.

Upon arriving, the hospital staff refused to admit the dying woman and asked Mother Teresa to leave and take the dying woman with her.

Refusing, Mother sat quietly in the waiting area, determined not to leave until the woman was admitted and cared for by the staff nurses and physicians. Finally, a doctor approached her and asked, "If we admit the woman, will you then leave?"

She agreed, and shortly she was on her way, and the woman, who just hours before was dying on the hot streets of Calcutta, being devoured by rats and insects, was taken care of by doctors and nurses.

It is interesting to note that Mother Teresa was almost forty years old when she stepped out alone into the slums of Calcutta. She had never done anything like this before that day.

In other words, she was just like us.

As Mother Teresa would often say, "Yesterday is gone; tomorrow has not yet come. We only have today. Let us begin."

Let us begin…

Let Us Begin

- Service to others is the "why" in the question, "Why are we here?"
- The longer we wait to begin a life of service, the longer we miss out on the joy it brings, and the more people in need suffer.
- Kindness is contagious. The kinder you are, the kinder you become, and you may very well see it in those around you.
- Helping untangle what binds others not only frees them but frees us of the things that bind us as well.
- Don't worry if people don't recall your name just as long as they remember you as the "nice one."

Chapter 6

THE END OF RANDOM
ACTS OF KINDNESS

I will see this day but once, if there's any kindness I can
show, let me show it now, for I'll never see this day again.
—Ronnie Gaylord

In the fall of 1972, country-recording artist Glen Campbell recorded
his twenty-third album, *Glen Travis Campbell*, featuring the single "I
Will Never Pass This Way Again." Detroit songwriter Ronnie Gaylord,
of the 1950s popular singing group the Gaylords, wrote this song that
became the anthem of what so many were longing for and reflected a
spirit that had been building for some time.

Campbell's song never rose any higher than number sixty-one in
the Billboard Top 100, but it did hit a timely and resonant tone during
a most turbulent time in the early 1970s that was still seeing protests
and unrest spilling over from the late 1960s.

As with so many times and movements in history, people began to
get weary—weary of the protests, hatred, and vitriolic rhetoric that had
been going on for nearly a decade. The battle for civil rights and the
war in Southeast Asia continued to drag on and were taking more and
more of a toll on so many.

People were looking for a change. All the demonstrations, hatred, speeches, and marches were only taking us so far. It was time to look for something more powerful than hate and force. It was time to look for something that could change the direction the world was taking. If all the things we had been doing had a limit effect, it was time to do something different.

Campbell's song may not have hit number one, but it took hold of a quiet revolution. The first two stanzas said it all:

> I will pass this way but once,
> if there's any good that I can do,
> let me do it now, for I'll never pass this way again.

> I will see this day but once,
> if there's any kindness I can show,
> let me show it now, for I'll never see this day again.

These words, as simple as they were, touched the hearts of those seeking to do just that—show kindness where they are and wherever they find themselves.

But these sentiments did not first see the light in 1972. They had been in existence for more than one hundred years, being widely circulated as a Quaker adage going back as far as 1859.

Its straightforward message was this:

"I expect to pass through this world but once. Any good, therefore, that I can do or any kindness I can show to any fellow creature, let me do it now. Let me not defer or neglect it, for I shall not pass this way again."

The first time I heard the phrase "random acts of kindness" was in a small book that a friend gave me with a picture of a cartoon gorilla on the cover that read "Gorilla Acts of Kindness" and set out with a number of examples on how to be kind to someone in performing random acts of kindness.

The axiom "random acts of kindness" is attributed to California writer Anne Herbert, who first wrote it on a placemat in 1982 after reading about "random acts of violence and senseless acts of cruelty."

In a world that is hungry for a philosophy that is brief enough to fit on a bumper sticker, this one certainly fits the bill. I am sure it prompted many to do random acts that hopefully helped others, and I am sure it made those committing those random acts feel pretty good about themselves.

The saying and the subsequent actions it may inspire seem to have the propensity to fall short with the first word—random.

It may look like a wonderful and romantic way to live your life, performing benevolent acts from time to time out of nowhere and riding off into the sunset like Fran Striker's Lone Ranger, with the person assisted standing in awe, asking, "Who was that masked man?"

Random acts of kindness only serve to touch a few of the many who are in need of help. The problem that I see comes in the very first word "random." Random is defined as proceeding, made, or occurring without definite aim, reason, or pattern.

It is also defined as a process of selection in which each item of a set has an equal probability of being chosen, lacking uniformity without continuous course, unknown, unidentified, or suspiciously out of place, odd or unpredictable.

A life of service to others cannot begin and end with a philosophy of random acts of kindness. If we truly want to find our real calling in reaching out to others, it cannot be found in skipping through our lives casually, doing kind deeds here and there, as a flower girl tosses rose petals as the bride walks down the aisle. That may make us feel better, but in doing so we may touch a few but miss the many who may need us most.

A life of service cannot be built on random acts of kindness. To have any lasting meaning and to have the tremendous power that a life of service can have to our community and the world at large, it has to be definite.

A life of service is full of intentional acts of kindness, those with a purpose, those that are done every day at every opportunity. By doing so, we find that it doesn't take long for it to become an ingrained part of our lives. The incidental becomes the essential.

We all must take care that as we reach out to those who are less fortunate that we do it for the right reasons. If it is just to make us feel good about ourselves and to give us a story to share with our friends and those we meet to show how altruistic we are and how much we care about others, we again are firing but missing the mark.

Saint Thomas Aquinas wrote that the intention of an act is every bit as important, if not more so, as the act itself.

Taking selfies of our good deeds and posting them diminishes what we have done. It is good to follow Jesus's advice to not let your right hand know what your left hand is doing.

On every desk in the Eblen Charities' Waddell Client Service Center, we have a five-by-seven-inch card that reads:

> Our job is not to judge.
> Our job is not to figure out
> if someone deserves something.
> Our job is to lift the fallen.
> to restore the broken, and to heal the hurting.

Longtime friend and Eblen Charities board member George Suggs sent those simple words to me; he thought they described the spirit and philosophy of our work at Eblen.

Framed in a plain black frame from the Dollar Tree, these cards provide a continual reminder to us not only why we are here but also how we are to see the wonderful families who come to us for help.

We see our job as not to figure out whom we are to help but rather to spend our time figuring out how we can help. It is not up to any of us to determine how deserving anyone is who is going through difficult times.

It is up to us to simply ask them how we can help and then find a way to do so. It is far from easy at times to put pieces together to help them find the relief they seek and to help them find a place in their lives where they can breathe, even for just a moment.

It is an honor to help these tremendous families and individuals who have the remarkable courage to get up each day and face the same battles that left them so exhausted the night before.

It is a great privilege to be able to share their lives and burdens, especially during their most difficult times. That, in itself, may also be a burden for those who reach out to help, but if it is, it is a glorious burden that we share.

One Tuesday afternoon a short time ago, a gentleman came into our office needing help with his electric bill. His power had been off for some time, and he had heard that if he came in, we might be able to get his power restored. He looked to be in his mid-sixties and couldn't have weighed more than 120 pounds, if that. He looked and dressed a lot like Uncle Si on *Duck Dynasty*.

After speaking with him and calling the power company, we were assured that his power would be turned on that afternoon. He thanked everyone, told us that he had to walk to our office, and it took him more than two hours, so he needed to get on his way to make it back home before dark.

One of our board members, Tim Gwennap, was working with clients that afternoon and had signed the gentleman in and had spoken to him for a while as he was waiting to been seen by one of our intake counselors. Knowing he was walking home, Tim gave him bus fare and thanked him for coming in, knowing that his power would be restored by the end of the day.

A few minutes after he left, the counselor who worked with him came into my office and told me the story of the gentleman they had just assisted. A few minutes after he left, an agent from the power company had called back and said the man's power would not be restored because she didn't get all the information she needed.

The counselor told her that was no problem; she had all the information and would be happy to give her whatever she needed. The agent, however, said she couldn't accept the information from us; she had to get it from the gentleman we were helping.

The counselor explained that he had already left and there was no way for us to get in touch with him. She again said we had all the information, which we had already shared with them. She also explained that we spoke to the power company dozens of times each day, assisting clients, and we had never encountered a problem.

Even so, the agent from the power company refused to restore our client's power as promised. We were concerned not only that the power company went back on their word to restore the electricity to our client's home but also that we had no way of letting him know, and he would be expecting his lights to be back on that evening.

I called our local representatives at the power company and left messages, but I did not hear back from them. I suggested to the counselor that she call the power company as if she had not spoken to them and start from scratch. If she had trouble again, she should ask to speak to a supervisor.

While we were discussing the best plan of action for us to take, Tim got in his car and set out to find the gentleman to bring him back to our office and let him know what was going on and to look for another way to help him.

Tim knew the direction he'd walked in, and even though Tim had given him bus fare, he figured that there was a good chance that he would save the money for something to eat and probably walk the nearly ten miles back home.

Tim drove up and down the roads that he knew our client would have to take to get back home, hoping that he had not taken the bus. He found him on his second round and brought him back to the office.

While Tim was searching for him, I went back to the counselor's office to see where we were. When I walked in she was still on the phone with the power company and had a big smile on her face. She looked up and said, "We got them back on."

Within a few minutes, Tim returned with the gentleman, still thinking that he might not have had his power restored and hoping to get him back on the phone to give the power company the information they needed. As they walked in the door, we told him the story of all that had happened and that his lights were back on.

He was very grateful, but as we drove him back home, he also seemed quite surprised that everyone would take the time and that the counselors and everyone at Eblen would put forth such an effort to help him and to search for him after he had left.

We explained to him that we were happy to do it and that he and what he was going through was every bit as important to us as it was to him. Tim also explained that we tried to do that for everyone who called upon us for help.

It is what we are honored to call our "Second-Mile Service." That is not stopping at just a minimum level of service and doing the best we can but giving all to everyone.

Almost everyone knows the saying about the second mile. In the Gospel of Matthew, Jesus told his disciples, "And whoever compels you to go one mile, go with him two" (Matthew 5:41).

There is an interesting story behind what Jesus told us to do. The Israelites, at the time of Jesus, were living in occupied territory. The Roman Empire ruled their land, and part of their law decreed that any Roman citizen could stop any Jew and compel him to stop whatever he was doing to carry the Roman's luggage (or whatever he was carrying) for one mile.

Apparently, Jesus knew the law, but, as unjust as it was, He did not say to disobey the law or launch some sort of protest or revolt. Instead, He instructed to turn the world on its ear with an amazing and intentional act of kindness.

He said that after you go the first mile that you are required by law, don't stop there. Go another mile, and know the second mile is ultimately different from the first.

The first mile you are forced by law to travel. The second mile you choose to go on your own. The first mile you are not in control, but the second mile that you travel, you choose to do. The entire paradigm shifts. The control on the second mile is now yours, not the one who forced you to drop everything to carry his load.

The second mile and the power of kindness change everything.

But the second mile should not be reserved for just a few—not for those chosen at random—but offered to all we have the privilege to meet.

If our Second-Mile Service had been given just at random, this gentleman might not have been helped with what he needed, and we might have missed the opportunity and joy we had in meeting him and the honor we had in serving.

We are asked this one question quite a bit: "Don't you ever get tired? Isn't it difficult to continue to do this every day with every person who calls on you to help?"

The answer is as simple as the work we do, and that answer is yes, but the answer and the feelings don't just stop there. Of course we all get weary, no matter how inspired any of us is in reaching out to others. The constant pressure and the responsibility can and does take a toll on us, and I am sure that is the same for everyone who reaches out to help those who are less fortunate, no matter how many or for how long.

What we have to do is keep reminding ourselves and encouraging each other that what we do is not about us. As tough as it may be for us on any given day, it is far tougher for those we serve.

At the end of our day, we get to go home and forget all, even if for just a few hours. We get to go home where it is warm, the lights are on, and there is food to eat. So many we see don't have what we so easily take for granted.

We are not here for ourselves. That is what should always joyfully be at the forefront of our minds and hearts.

We must do what we think we cannot do. And we must do it together.

There is more than an occasional day when we think, *I cannot return one more phone call or talk to one more client.* In those times we try to put ourselves in our client's place and ask, "What if I was the one on the other end of the phone or had come all this way for help and had to wait or come back because someone was too tired to see me?" I also think about what Mother Teresa did for so long and the way in which she once answered that question.

Early in 1969, the British Broadcasting Corporation sent veteran journalist, author, and television personality Malcolm Muggeridge, along with a cameraman and a producer, to Calcutta to do an hour-long documentary on Mother Teresa's work, following her as she served the poor and the dying in the streets.

A year before, Mother Teresa had met Muggeridge while in the United Kingdom. She was visiting the coworkers of the first Missionaries of Charity in England, which was begun by a group of women who had visited her previously in Calcutta.

Oliver Hunkin, the director of religious programming for the British Broadcasting Corporation, came to Muggeridge, assigning him to conduct a short interview with this unknown nun from Calcutta. At the time, Muggeridge had never heard of Mother Teresa and thought it was most certainly a waste of his time.

Mother Teresa was as reluctant to be interviewed for Muggeridge's Sunday evening *Meeting Point* program for many of the same reasons he had and also for the fact that she didn't like to do interviews in general. She avoided the limelight for herself, as she saw herself just "a pencil in God's hand" and that He wrote what He wanted.

She was not the story. The work was, but even so, Mother Teresa felt that any coverage of her work was unnecessary.

At the interview she was a most visibly anxious Mother Teresa and answered Malcolm's questions hesitantly and in a quiet, faltering voice. Muggeridge had little patience for this tiny woman who arrived late for the interview and whom he had initially thought was Indian (he learned of her Albanian heritage during the interview but had no interest in talking to her about it).

He led Mother Teresa through a number of basic questions as she talked about her work and avoided any questions about herself and made it a point not to ask for any contributions. They finished the interview with neither being impressed with the other. Within days of the May 1968 broadcast, as much as forty-five thousand dollars was contributed to the Missionaries of Charity to continue their work.

Mother Teresa's simple message touched the hearts of many of those who watched. The BBC was besieged by requests to re-air the interview, drawing even more donations.

At first, Mother Teresa was reluctant to meet with the journalist again and have him and his crew come out at all. But after a while she agreed to let them in to see the work of the Missionaries of Charity firsthand.

This interview would be nothing like the first. They would not be seated in a pristine BBC studio. It wouldn't be where Muggeridge was most comfortable; it would be where Mother Teresa was most comfortable.

It would be in the streets of Calcutta, amid the poverty, disease, squalor, garbage, and decadence of those existing in the worst slums the world has ever seen. There would be no easy or entertaining answers to what Malcolm and his crew were witnessing; it was simply love in action—something that so many talk about but so few actually do.

What turned the world-weary journalist around was what he saw in Mother Teresa's face. The deep love that he saw radiating from her as she bathed the lepers and picked up the dying was nothing this war-hardened professional journalist had ever encountered.

His interview began with this simple question:

"Do you do this every day?"

"Oh yes," Mother Teresa answered. "It is my mission. It is how I serve and love my Lord."

"How long have you been doing this? How many months?"

"Months?" replied Mother Teresa. "Not months but years. Maybe eighteen years."

"Eighteen years!" Muggeridge asked, "You have been working in the streets for eighteen years?"

"Yes," Mother Teresa answered, "It is my privilege to be here. These are my people. These are the ones who my Lord has given me to love."

"Do you ever get tired? Do you ever feel like quitting and letting someone else take over your ministry? After all, you are beginning to get older."

"Oh no, this is where the Lord wants me, and this is where I am happy to be. I feel young when I am here. The Lord is good to me. How privileged I am to serve Him."

In the simplicity of that brief conversation, a heart and a life were indelibly changed—the life of Malcolm Muggeridge. "I will never forget that little lady as long as I live. The face, the glow, the eyes, and the love—it was all so pure and so beautiful. I shall never forget it. It was like being in the presence of an angel. It changed my life. I have not been the same person since. It is more than I can describe."

It was that one simple question and the example that shone above all. It is not easy, but then again, it is not supposed to be. But with this great effort comes a great joy that cannot be found anywhere else.

"I do this every day. I am privileged to serve …"

Let us begin …

Let Us Begin

- There are only so many tomorrows. Whatever good we can do, we cannot wait. We must do it now.
- A life of service cannot be lived at random. We must look for intentional acts of kindness to reach all we meet.
- Our job is never to judge; instead, it is to lift the fallen, restore the broken, and heal the hurting.
- Live a life of second-mile service in reaching out to those in need. Always look to go a step further from where you currently are or are willing to go.
- We are not here for ourselves. We are here in the service of others.

Chapter 7

FINDING YOUR CALLING

The place God calls you to is the place where your
deep gladness and the world's deep hunger meet.
—Frederick Buechner

Samuel Clemens, writing under his famous pen name, Mark Twain, has
been attributed to what many think is the most poignant and thought-
provoking words ever quoted.

It wasn't one of his acclaimed novels, such as *Huckleberry Finn, The
Adventures of Tom Sawyer,* or *A Connecticut Yankee in King Arthur's
Court,* nor did it come from any of his short stories or chronicles of his
world travels.

The simple quote is this:

"The two most important days in your life are the day you are born
and the day you find out why."

In an earlier chapter I mentioned how my grandfather used to tell
me that to find true happiness in my life was to find a need and fill it
He would tell me almost daily, as I recall, to "Pray for your vocation,
and you will find what you are supposed to do, and when you do you
will find out who you are."

Now, *vocation* was a new word to me but one I learned the meaning
of and the great importance it held very quickly.

The word *vocation* comes from a Latin word meaning "summons" or to "call." The definition of vocation in English Oxford Dictionary dictionaries is a strong feeling of suitability for a particular career or occupation.

Again, what I trust that Grandpa was trying to tell me was that instead of looking to lead our lives, we should look to where our lives will lead us. He was directing me to discover that the most important answers in life are not found within us but rather on what is around us—what God puts before us to do.

I understood that my grandfather was telling me—pretty much on a daily basis—that a vocation was the most important thing we can find. He believed that we all have one; it is just a matter of finding it.

Calling to mind, once again, the thought of "Find out why."

So if there is a calling for us, there must be someone or something that is doing the calling.

But how do we do that when so many voices call out to us and so many things demand our attention, all claiming to be our true mission?

From my earliest days, I understood that this thing Grandpa kept talking to me about was far more than any ordinary occupation I might find. It was not about only what I was to do with my life but who I was to become.

He also took a great amount of time making sure that I understood that a vocation might not always be the same as a profession or a career that someone might choose.

Professions, jobs, or careers, he explained, are what we all do to provide for our families and ourselves and hopefully give back in some manner to the communities in which we live. The career paths we choose don't always have to be what we see as our vocations. We all have many interests and talents that we offer and pursue that may be totally separate from what our true vocations are.

I have had the pleasure of working with Bill Waddell for nearly twenty years. Bill has an amazing life and career, and spent the greater part of his working life as one of the top salesmen of a major industrial supply company. Bill later founded his own successful industrial supply company, as well as other business interests. He could sell three-day-old ice.

It seems everyone knows Bill, and it most certainly seems he knows everyone. He forged a wonderful life for his wife, Mary Dot, and his two daughters, Beth and Tina, thanks to his skills as a salesman and the service and kindness he showed to all.

But his profession was far from his true vocation. He touched countless lives with his generosity and compassion to everyone he met, and before long he quickly was seen as one of the people in our community who would listen to those in need and offer tireless help, not only to those who sought him out but to anyone he heard of who might need assistance.

Joe Eblen brought Bill by the Charities office for us to meet. That day he showed me within the first few minutes who he was and what his vocation was and is.

When Bill and Joe walked in, I was on the phone with a friend who was working in the HR department at the Grove Park Inn. She had called us to see if we could help a little boy who was very ill. The family was having difficulty because they lived at the end of a rough, unpaved road. The nurses and medical personnel who needed to get to their house could not make it down their road at times.

My friend asked if there was anything we could do to get this mile-long road to be passable. I was making notes when Bill came in. Having heard my conversation he asked me what I was working on. I quickly told him the story, and he asked if I minded if he talked to my friend.

Bill asked a few questions, made a few notes, and asked if he could call them back. After he hung up, he told me that he knew someone in the gravel business, and he would ask him if he would donate the gravel and help fix the road.

An hour or so later, Bill came back and told us that it was all set—the company would go out there the next day and fix the road so the visiting nurses and other medical services that were so vital for this little one-year-old boy and his family could get to their home.

Bill took action right away. He didn't have to study the problem or convene a group to study the problem or bring others in to tackle the problem. He made one call and asked for help for this family. Within twenty-four hours, he had the road repaired.

As wonderful as this was, sadly, the little boy only lived a few more weeks, but for those few short weeks he was able to get the care he so desperately needed, greatly because Bill walked in the office that day and wasted no time in offering help.

I was quick to learn, long before I ever found out what he did as a profession, that he had been doing what I witnessed all of his life. He continues to do this to this day, helping all who call with everything from helping build ramps, to finding refrigerators, washers, and dryers and all manner of other assistance at the Eblen Charities Waddell Client Service Center, which was named for him.

His vocation is without question. It is to help those less fortunate with whatever they may need, and he has been able to use the connections and experience he gained throughout his career to assist those who are experiencing darker days.

When we talk about vocation, we are not so much talking about ourselves in a manner that asks, "What do I want to do?" but rather, "What is it that I am supposed to do with my life? What is it that God wants me to do?"

As mentioned earlier, the most important questions we can ask are, "What is it that the world needs, and what can I offer?" And whatever the answers are to those questions are what guide our lives and open the door to true happiness and joy.

Being called to be a mother, father, or grandparent is every bit as important as being called to be a doctor, nurse, teacher, or minister. But whatever it is we are called to do, we are the only ones who can do what must be done.

Others may be able to do similar things, but there is no one who can do what we are called to do exactly how we do it. We bring to our callings unique talents, perspectives, experiences, and thoughts that make our callings, even though many may share them, distinctive to us.

I do believe that we all can experience the second greatest day of our lives and find out the reasons why we were born. I do believe that to find out our "why" is more up to us than to anyone or anything else.

As Jack London once wrote in a 1905 essay, *Getting Into Print*, "Don't loaf and invite inspiration; light out after it with a club, and if you don't get it you will nonetheless get something that looks remarkably like it." In other words, it is up to us to discover our reasons that we are placed on this earth. We must hunt them down, if need be. But when we find them, we and the world around us will be much better for our efforts.

If we look around us, as Mother Teresa wrote to the young lady who wanted to join her in Calcutta, we can find our "whys"—we can find our own Calcutta. And if we keep looking and paying close attention, at some point we will find out just why we are here.

It is then we truly will come alive and begin to live. Our purposes and passions come together to not only inspire our lives but also to light the lives of all with whom we come in contact.

Some of us may find our purposes early on. For many of us, they may take us on a journey to get us ready for what our callings are. Our callings are there all along, but that doesn't always mean we are ready for them. There are times when we will have a lot to learn, skills to acquire and hone, and an understanding we may not always have to begin our lives of purpose as of yet.

Saint Paul found his purpose on the road to Damascus. C. S. Lewis found his purpose after decades of study and searching. Mozart composed symphonies at the age of ten. Harry Truman served as a soldier and owned and ran a men's clothing store well into his adulthood before becoming a county commissioner and entering the US Senate after turning fifty years old, becoming president at sixty, and ending World War II.

Mozart found his "why" early. Truman found his much later, after a long journey as a failed haberdasher in Kansas City, Missouri, to the most powerful man in the world, stopping the Axis powers and saving democracy and freedom. Was Truman ready for this monumental task at the age of thirty-five or forty? Probably not. But his calling was the same, and at sixty he changed and saved the world.

Once we see why we are here, we can begin to fulfill the purpose of our lives. We may have to exercise patience, but we must never stop looking, never stop paying attention to all that is around us, and never, ever stop preparing for what it is we eventually find.

Abraham Lincoln spent his entire life rebounding from failure after failure to eventually becoming the sixteenth president of the United States, ending slavery, and preserving the United States. He was reported to say, "If I had eight hours to chop down a tree, I would spend six hours sharpening the ax." And he remarked, "I will study and get ready, and perhaps my chance will come." His did, as so will ours if we keep looking and are open to it.

We all hear a lot about fate and that we all have a destiny. I believe that our lives are affected and directed by our decisions and our actions. If we are truly wise, we will see how things in our lives evolve as we keep looking for our callings.

Looking back at where we have been and what may have brought us to a certain point in our lives can also serve to part the curtains as to where our callings lie. Where we have been is every bit as important as where we are going; it is what has brought us to where we are. Whether times were good or difficult, they served to bring us to where we are and closer to our vocations.

There is no doubt that we all will struggle with our purposes for being here at one point or another in our lives. Everyone—every organization, company, team, and entity—seeks to find relevance in the world.

I wonder if so many of us miss our vocations for so long because we are looking for something beyond what we may already be doing. Perhaps we have missed seeing the callings because we are not looking at them through the right set of eyes or through the depths of our hearts.

In 1963 President John F. Kennedy visited the space center in Houston, Texas. He toured the facility that he put into overdrive by giving the directive of landing a man on the moon and bringing him back safely to earth by the end of the decade.

The president visited each department; he talked with the engineers, scientists, and directors, asking them about their jobs and their thoughts on the program. When he was leaving, he spotted a custodian mopping the floor.

He asked the group that was with him to wait, and he walked up to the custodian and introduced himself.

"And what do you do here?" he asked.

"I am helping to put a man on the moon, Mr. President," he replied.

What a wonderful attitude. This gentleman, who I am sure was ignored by many who thought his job was far less important than theirs, saw that what he was doing was part of a much bigger picture. Everyone was there to put a man on the moon.

The custodian saw what so many missed. He saw what he was already doing as his vocation—his calling. And that was to do his part to answer the president's call and challenge to put a man on the moon by the end of the decade and to bring him back safely to earth. In that valiant effort, no job was menial.

There is a well-known story of three stone masons who were laboring diligently in the construction of a cathedral.

On a foggy autumn day nearly eight hundred years ago, a traveler happened upon a large group of workers adjacent to the River Avon.

Despite being overdue for an important rendezvous, curiosity convinced the traveler that he should inquire about their work.

With a slight detour he moved toward the first of the three tradesmen and said, "My dear fellow, what is it that you are doing?"

The man continued his work and grumbled, "I am cutting stones."

Realizing that the mason did not wish to engage in a conversation, the traveler moved toward the second of the three and repeated the question.

To the traveler's delight, this time the man stopped his work, ever so briefly, and stated that he was a stonecutter. He then added, "I came to Salisbury from the north to work but as soon as I earn ten quid [ten dollars] I will return home."

The traveler thanked the second mason, wished him a safe journey home and began to head to the third of the trio.

When he reached the third worker he once again asked the original question. This time the worker paused, glanced at the traveler until they made eye contact, and then looked skyward, drawing the traveler's eyes upward.

The third mason replied, "I am a mason, and I am building a cathedral." He continued, saying, "I have journeyed many miles to be part of those who are constructing this magnificent cathedral. I have spent many months away from my family, and I miss them dearly. However, I know how important Salisbury Cathedral will be one day, and I know how many people will find sanctuary and solace here. I know this because the bishop once told me his vision for this great place. He described how people would come from all parts to worship here."

He also told the traveler that the cathedral would not be completed in their days but that the future depended on their hard work. He paused and then said, "So I am prepared to be away from my family because I know it is the right thing to do. I hope that one day my son will continue in my footsteps and perhaps even his son, if need be."

Isn't it interesting that all three men were doing the same job and saw their labor in different ways? The first saw his work only as a laborious job of "cutting stones." To him there was nothing more to it, just back-breaking work. The second was only there for a payday. He was there to earn his ten dollars and head back home, possibly not to return or at least not until he needed another ten dollars.

It was the third stonemason who found his calling in what the others saw as menial and degrading work. The first two looked at it with their eyes and felt it only through their muscle, sinew, and aching backs. The last one looked at it with his heart and spirit.

He found his purpose in the work he was already doing and found not only the reason for his life on earth but, according to the story, had a spirit of gratitude in being able to be part of the building of such a place where so many would find solace and sanctuary. To him this wasn't just "cutting stones." To him he was getting to be part of so much more; he was building a cathedral.

In an earlier chapter I shared a bit about Mother Teresa and what brought her to become the Saint of the Gutters. Her calling to serve the poorest of the poor—what she so movingly deemed as her "call within a call"—came after decades of teaching young girls in the Loreto convent.

When arriving in Calcutta she continued to teach the children of the city by giving them their lessons by writing in the dirt with a stick in any space she could find. No Nobel Peace Prize, no looming sainthood, no global recognition and admiration, just one lone, diminutive nun who was nearly forty years old, teaching children in the slums and degradation of one of the worst places on earth.

She knew in her heart of hearts and her soul of souls that she was not just "cutting stones" but building a cathedral.

So I'll ask you what I ask myself: what cathedral are you building today?

There is one waiting to be built.

You will find it where what you need to do most intersects with what the world most needs to be done.

Let us begin …

Let Us Begin

- One of the most important days in our lives is when we find out why we are born.
- Our callings may not always be what we do for a living. They very well may be found in "a call within a call."
- Instead of asking ourselves, "What can the world give to me?" we should ask, "What is it I can give to the world?"
- Don't wait for inspiration; go after it.
- We can find our callings at any time in our lives. We should never stop looking or stop preparing for them.

Chapter 8

A PENCIL IN GOD'S HAND

No one is useless in this world who lightens the burden of another.
—Charles Dickens

Throughout her life, anytime someone would compliment or mention her work, Mother Teresa was quick to say, "I am a little pencil in God's hands. He does the thinking. He does the writing. He does everything and sometimes it is really hard because it is a broken pencil, and He has to sharpen it a little more."

"It is not my work; it is God's work," she would kindly correct anyone who wanted to talk about her and the work of the Missionaries of Charity. She knew, even in the gaze of the spotlight's eye and with an entire world watching her and hanging on her every word and action, that her human fragility and limitations would only hinder any good work that she could do. Mother Teresa was a living example of what Saint Paul wrote in Philippians 4:13, "I can do all things through Christ who gives me strength."

All work is God's work, as my grandfather would always remind me. No matter what it is you are doing—washing dishes, sweeping a walkway, driving a cab, or performing heart surgery—everything we do, how we do it, and what kindness and love we bring to it matters.

A few years ago I was in Waterloo, Iowa, at the National Wrestling

Hall of Fame's Dan Gable Museum for their Hall of Fame inductions. One afternoon I was talking with Dan, and as we were catching up, he mentioned our work at Eblen and that we were doing "God's work."

I told him that all that he accomplished as an athlete—national, world, and Olympic champion, as well as an unparalleled coaching career—was just as much God's work as anything we were doing at Eblen.

As we continued to talk, I explained that if it hadn't been for him and the fact that I had been a big fan of his from his days at Iowa State and through his 1972 record-setting Olympic victory in Munich and his incredible coaching career, I never would have wrestled and would have never learned the principles and tenets that wrestling taught. The determination, the discipline, the mental toughness, and how to get off your back all contributed greatly to our outreach to those in need.

But I didn't only learn from his victories. I learned just as much from his sole defeat in college, breaking his 181 high school and college match winning streak at the 1970 NCAA Wrestling Championships. It was how he responded to that one loss and how it propelled him to work even harder, winning the world title the next year and Olympic gold the year after that.

What I learned from Dan, George Scott, Lou Thesz, and Jack and Gerald Brisco in my very early years all culminated in what I found many years later in assisting others.

In his biography, *I Never Had it Made*, the great baseball player Jackie Robinson, who broke the color barrier in major league sports, once said, "A life is not important except in the impact it has on other lives."

Of course, there was no way that he or the others would have known what a lasting influence they had on my life and that of countless others. We may never know the effect our actions and lives have on others.

All work is important, so never minimize what you may be doing, for you never know whom you may be influencing or the effect your kindness, actions, and example will have.

As we continue to search for our callings or slow down enough for us to see them, there are a few things we should keep in mind about what a vocation really is.

First of all, I think that so many of us may miss our callings by our constant search, believing that there may only be one specific profession or vocation out there for us.

There may be a number of vocations for which we are suited or called to do. We may squander so much of our precious time that we could be working within our callings by looking for another one that we think we would prefer.

Remember Mother Teresa's first vocation was as a cloistered Loreto sister. She later saw her vocation as a teacher and then her well-known "call within a call" to serve Calcutta's wretched poor.

Later, she saw an even larger calling in founding the Missionaries of Charity and serving as, albeit reluctantly, leader and voice of those who never had a chance to speak for themselves. No matter where her calling led, she was always first and foremost a teacher.

If you believe or are even open to believe that all work is important, then any job can be part of our vocations. The job itself may not be a vocation, but it may supply the means for us to pursue our true calling.

Years ago, I was fortunate enough to teach a number of classes as an adjunct instructor with the Duke University Nonprofit Management Program. One class was on developing public-private partnerships, and during a class discussion, one of the participants asked me if I thought that working for a nonprofit was more important or nobler than working for a for-profit company.

I told her that I didn't think so. I thought that working for both the public and private sector was equally significant. She wasted no time in telling me how wrong I was and how insulted she was that I would have the audacity to say that or even to think such a thing.

She went on to tell me that she worked for a battered women's shelter and that was far more important than anyone who delivered oil or drove a Pepsi truck.

In response, I said the work that she was doing in her community was invaluable and that she should be very happy she was able to make a living in helping so many in such desperate times in their lives.

But so was the work of everyone in her community. I said that I thought she shouldn't think the work of those who worked in the private sector was less significant than the tremendous work that she was doing.

"Does your organization pay taxes?" I asked her.

"No, of course not," she said, looking at me like I was a bigger idiot than she first thought.

"Do you know why your organization doesn't have to pay taxes?"

"Because we are a nonprofit."

I expected that her next question to me was going to be the one that Dorothy posed to the scarecrow when she first met him on her way to Oz: "And what would you do if you did have a brain?"

"Yes," I said, "but also because the companies we are talking about do pay taxes so nonprofits don't.

"The federal government thinks that nonprofits can do the work we all do more effectively than they can, so part of their help is that we don't have to pay taxes on our revenue.

"But that is only part of it," I continued. "We are able to operate as we do partially because the private sector does pay taxes."

Then I asked her one final question. "Do any for-profit companies support the great work you do? Does Pepsi or an oil company or any other company donate to you with cash or any in-kind donations?"

"Of course they do. We have some very generous donors."

"You are again very fortunate, but that being the case, why would you think what they do is not as important as what you do? Without them you may have a difficult time maintaining your work. We all would. That is why I think their work is every bit as important as ours. We all work together."

I really don't think my explanation helped much as she was still pretty angry for the rest of the class, as I remember. In fact, at the end of the class she filled out her survey and gave the room we were in a score of ten for the facility and gave me a one for the content and instruction value (with ten being the highest and one being the lowest—just in case you were wondering).

This conversation also brought me back to think about vocations and all work being holy—not so much about those who work in the public sector but those who work in the for-profit world.

Their jobs may have been driving a truck, fixing people's teeth, or selling homes, but that only served their vocations on reaching out to battered women, helping children learn, or providing assistance in countless other ways to those in need. There cannot be one without the other.

All vocations are important. We cannot look down on someone else's calling because we believe ours are nobler or more important. Arrogance and ego have no place in our callings. They diminish us and the work that we are called to do.

There are no lower or higher callings. As with the stone cutters, it is all how we view the world and our places in it.

In a recent article on the popular website the Art of Manliness, a survey discussed an interesting fact—that the demarcation between vocations, professions, and jobs viewed by those who hold them seem to all be alike, no matter what they may be. One-third of the doctors questioned saw their work as a job, while one-third of the sanitation workers saw their work as a vocation. It is a matter of our hearts' perceptions.

So how can we see what our vocations are? We know that they are not always the same as what we do for a living. No matter what our jobs may be, I think this is good to remember and will inspire us to move forward and see that our true vocation is what we bring to what we do; it is not just what we do.

Years ago it was not unusual for a person to spend his or her entire working life at one company. In more recent years, the average person of the baby boomer generation has seen job changes up to eleven times before he or she retires, with the new generations on track for even more. In the fast-paced and constantly changing world, it seems, more and more, having a single job for life is a thing of the past.

But the one thing that does not change is the calling that we have. That is what we take with us and offer to others, no matter where we find ourselves or what we do for a living. Recognizing what our gifts are and seeking how we can use them to help others will move us toward our vocations.

Recently I met the manager of an Ashley HomeStore here in Asheville. We met at four o'clock in the morning to set up for our annual WLOS-TV Spring Clean Coat Drive to benefit Eblen Charities. Long before dawn, Jeff Patton, Lauren Brigman, a number of WLOS folks, and volunteers set up tents, and assembled boxes provided by my friend Todd Campbell of Two Men and a Truck on that chilly April morning.

The Spring Clean Coat Drive was the idea of WLOS-TV's Guy Chancey and Estee Felton as a way to collect coats and help keep thousands of children and adults warm during the winters in the western North Carolina mountains each year.

Ashley HomeStore had extended their kindness and the use of their store and parking lot for us to collect coats.

As hundreds of generous people drove up throughout the day to donate their gently used and new coats, Jeff and I had a chance to get acquainted. He told me about his career and the various jobs he had and the places he lived throughout his career.

Jeff asked me about our work at Eblen. He told me that he appreciated the work that we did, and he wished that he could do more of that type of work. He went on to tell me of a great many wonderful things he, his wife, and their daughters had done in the many places they had lived.

Our conversation turned to vocations, as again he referenced the work of Eblen Charities. Jeff has a kind and gentle sprit that is evident as you meet him. His calming voice and his temperate manner put all he comes into contact with at ease. I was impressed with how he greeted and thanked everyone who brought their coats by, speaking quietly and respectfully to everyone as he helped them carry their coats to our collection tables.

I remarked at how well he interacted with all who came to his store and asked if there ever was a time that he got frustrated with customers and if his kind demeanor helped when he ran into a disgruntled customer.

He quickly told me that he was no different from anyone else. He tried to always realize that whomever he was talking to might have a problem and that there was likely more than met the eye.

Jeff shared a story about a woman who had called him with a complaint she had about the furniture delivery she had just received. As she vented, Jeff listened patiently and discerned that it really wasn't the delivery that she was having trouble with; she was just having a terrible day.

As he talked to her, she began to calm down a bit and realized that maybe her displeasure with Jeff wasn't really bothering her so much at all. She thanked him for listening to her, for helping her with her request, and for being so kind and helping her feel better after such a trying day.

"You know," I said to Jeff, "I think that is what your calling is."

"What?" he asked me, looking at me like I might have grown another head.

"How you make people feel when you talk to them. You have an amazing gift to bring to so many."

"What gift is that?"

"Your kindness and caring brings peace to those you meet or those who come across your path, just by the way you talk and listen to them. Selling furniture and managing this huge store has positioned you in a wonderful place."

He smiled a bit as we continued our conversation.

"I can't believe that you haven't heard this from anyone before. It's not what you do here that is the most important thing; the gifts and talents that you have been given that you bring with you every day is why you are here," I added.

We also talked about what a great thing he and his staff were doing in providing furniture and accessories to his customers. When my friend Bill Waddell (whom I have the pleasure of working with and mentioned earlier) was recovering from a stroke, he needed a reclining chair to help him rest and to get up and down more easily. Bill's two daughters, Beth and Tina, came to Ashley's, and Jeff personally worked with them to find just the right chair and got it to Bill that same day.

What he did was not just selling a chair to a customer; he helped a family he had just met get through a difficult time and helped Bill with his recovery. Jeff and Ashley helped a wonderful family dealing with a tough situation breathe a bit easier and left them with one less thing to worry about.

It was great to see Bill meet Jeff at the coat drive and not know that he was the one who got him the chair. When they were introduced to each other and I told him the story, he and Jeff looked at each other and said in unison, "That was you?" and they hugged each other.

What we talked about was the vocation that he and his staff had and that furniture was only a very small part of what they do and what they offer to our community.

They help provide a comfortable home for so many—a place where their customers can unwind after a hard day, a place where they can find solace from the craziness of the outside world, and a place where their children have safe and warm beds and a table on which they can eat. Not only that but he also provides jobs to those who work for him so they can take care of their families.

He is building a cathedral. Furniture is just a way to do it. There is no greater calling.

In meeting and getting to know Jeff, I thought of one thing we all share in whatever our callings may be, and that is reaching out and showing kindness to all with whom we are fortunate to come into contact. That is something we can all do no matter what our talents are or where our callings lie.

Mother Teresa knew this most of all. She said constantly that the greatest poverty of all was not a lack of material things but rather the need of love and to know that someone cared about them, cared for them.

One afternoon I was in our lobby and heard someone call out, "Hi, Bill, how have you been?" I looked around and saw a very thin, tired-looking gentleman who was waiting for one of our intake counselors to finish a call on his behalf, to help him keep his lights and electricity from being disconnected.

He asked me if I remembered him and if I had a few minutes to talk with him. I told him that I certainly remembered him and that

I had all the time that he wanted for us to talk. He explained that he had been doing better since the last time he had visited us and that he now just needed a little help as he had gotten behind in his power bill.

He had not asked for help for some time. His son had just moved back in with him, and his limited income had been strained all the more. He was now in danger of not only losing his power but also being further behind by having to pay his past due bill and a reconnection fee.

He couldn't find help anywhere else, but it seemed he came to Eblen hoping for more than just assistance in paying his power bill.

We spent time talking about his family and what he had been doing since the last time I had seen him. He was certainly worried about his utility bill, but he seemed to just want to talk.

He seemed more worried about feeling alone in his situation than the dollar amount that would keep him with electricity. I believe his fear of loneliness brought him to us as much as his financial need.

In talking with him, I was reminded of a story I had read that Mother Teresa wrote about a different kind of poverty, one that invades the heart as deeply as the lack of means invades physical lives.

As Mother Teresa reminds us, abandonment is an awful poverty.

> One day I visited a house where our sisters shelter the aged. This is one of the nicest houses in England, filled with beautiful and precious things, yet there was not one smile on the faces of these people. All of them were looking toward the door.

> I asked the sister in charge, "Why are they like that? Why can't you see a smile on their faces?" I am accustomed to seeing smiles on people's faces. I think a smile generates a smile, just as love generates love.

> The sister answered, "The same thing happens every day. They are always waiting for someone to come and visit them. Loneliness eats them up, and day after day they do not stop looking. Nobody comes."

Abandonment is an awful poverty. There are poor people everywhere, but the deepest poverty is not being loved. The poor we seek may live near us or far away. They can be materially or spiritually poor.

They may be hungry for bread or hungry for friendship. They may need clothing, or they may need the sense of wealth that God's love for them represents. They may need the shelter of a house made of bricks and cement or the shelter of having a place in our hearts.

I continually stand in amazement of the wonderful staff we have at Eblen Charities and so many I have met throughout the world for the compassion, time, and love they offer in serving all who call upon them in their times of need. Their job is far from easy. Our community would be so much poorer without them.

I am even more amazed at the courage it must take our families to come in or call organizations, seeking help for food, to stay in their homes, purchase their medication, and other challenges they may have in their times of need.

But through all this, we must continue to reach out to the "poverty of the heart" that so many of us have, regardless of our financial situations.

We don't have to look far to find it, nor do we have to do much more than smile and spend a few minutes talking to those we meet to begin to lighten their hearts and ours.

This is a calling that we all share. This is where we find our own Calcutta.

Let us begin …

Let Us Begin

- Your calling in life may not be glamorous, but it is your calling nonetheless. You are the only one who can do it. That is why you are called.
- Keep your mind and heart open. You may find your vocation in a totally different direction than where you started.
- Value everyone's work. All work is important, no matter what it may be.
- Beware of falling into an attitude of self-righteousness. Never think your calling is more important than others'.
- Begin your kindness with a smile and a kind word to everyone with whom you come in contact.

Chapter 9

FINDING CALCUTTA

Never worry about numbers. Help one person at a time
and always start with the person nearest you.
—Mother Teresa of Calcutta

In thinking about vocations, I suppose a simple way to define them would be as something we do, not for any gain but for the work itself, the good that it does for others, and the impact it has on those around us. It is not work for work's sake; it is work that makes the lives of those we come into contact with better.

Our callings utilize our talents and gifts in ways that touch others, help them through difficult times, and let them know they are not alone. I believe that all callings, no matter what they are, have the same heart, the same core value, and that is simply kindness.

We are all called to be kind and to live our lives in service to others. It is because showing kindness is something we all can do at all times.

It is not reserved for those who are wealthy, well educated, or have a particular position or talent. It is something that we all can do, and the more we do it, the easier it becomes. One kind deed can move us to other actions that are even greater and may open our eyes to our true callings.

Kindness, it has been said, is the language that the deaf can hear and the blind can see. Kindness may well indeed be the only universal language.

Throughout my life I have been most fortunate to have met a great number of wonderful people whose kindness still resonates with me so many years later. Their examples have inspired me, even today, to do better and keep looking for ways to share what I have with everyone I meet.

Cookie Mills is one of those people.

The morning I was going to have lunch with my friend, Cookie Mills, I found another quote from three-time world heavyweight boxing champion Muhammad Ali. It read, "Impossible is just a big word thrown around by small men who find it easier to live in the world they've been given than to explore the power they have to change it. Impossible is not a fact. It's an opinion. Impossible is not a declaration. It's a dare. Impossible is potential. Impossible is temporary. Impossible is nothing."

Muhammad Ali always was someone I admired. From his dedication and sacrifice in winning an Olympic gold medal to capturing the world title on three separate occasions to his philanthropic work around the world, Ali certainly personified what he said about the word "impossible."

The same can be said for Cookie Mills and his Ducker Road Council. Cookie found his own Calcutta, not by traveling around the world but by looking out his own front door.

William Mills, or "Cookie," as his many friends and admirers affectionately call him, is just a bit past his mid-sixties and is now into his second decade of touching the lives of so many people for whom others have long given up on and turned their backs.

"I only thought I would be doing this for three or four months and move on to something else," Cookie said, shaking his head, "but there still are those who are trying so hard and still need help."

The Ducker Road community is located in Skyland, North Carolina, just outside of the Asheville city limits. Predominately an African American community, it had slowly fallen into disarray as many of the families that had made it a wonderful neighborhood to raise a family in the sixties and seventies had moved away.

Drug dealers moved in and set up shop, selling their wares to others who moved in or to those who knew that Ducker Street was now the place to go in South Asheville.

Families were afraid to leave their homes and let their children or grandchildren go outside to play. Eventually, the entire street became overgrown with weeds, trash, and abandoned appliances, surrounding the good families who refused to be pushed out from their homes and the community they loved.

Cookie grew up on Ducker Road. He was the ninth of ten children. His father was a logger, and his mother worked in the lunchroom at Valley Springs Elementary School. She would bring home whatever food was left at the end of each school day and, along with the food they raised, would feed her family.

After graduating from T. C. Roberson High School, Cookie went to work at Magnavox as a press operator. Always industrious, Cookie also kept the job he'd had since his early days in high school—cutting lawns in the evening and on weekends.

One of his clients, the personnel director of Carolina Power and Light, offered Cookie a job as a meter reader. He took him up on the offer and moved through the ranks, spending twelve years as a lineman, twelve years as a supervisor, and finishing his thirty-four-year career with the last ten as a senior support specialist.

Cookie, his wife, and their sons were living just a few blocks from Ducker Road, but he drove the road every day, to and from work. What he saw on a daily basis troubled him greatly, as he witnessed drug deals and other activities that kept the families—those he'd grown up with and loved—hostages in their own homes.

This was Cookie's Calcutta.

"I wanted to do something but didn't know what to do," Cookie told me. "How could I do anything? I was just one person. I never went to college, but there I was, seeing my old neighborhood being run by drug dealers and junkies.

"Every day I saw what was happening and [wondered] why no one was doing anything. But I couldn't say much because I wasn't doing anything either.

"But every time I thought of that, I kept hearing what my father always told all of us and that was not to let people tell you what you can do—show people what you can do."

So on June 29, 2004, Cookie wrote, printed, and distributed thirty-two homemade brochures titled "Cancer on Ducker Road," announcing a community meeting the next week. Much to Cookie's surprise, thirty families showed up, many thinking that it was Cookie who had cancer and needed the support of his friends.

Not knowing what to say or even where to begin, he began to talk about what was going on in their community and that the cancer was not his but was affecting all of them. The cancer was the drugs being brought into the community. The cancer was prevailing itself on the children and young people in their community, along with a "learned helplessness" that was growing daily as part of their culture.

"Our kids deserve better," Cookie told the group. Hearing what this meeting was about and what Cookie had in mind, some walked out, while others stayed and joined the conversation to figure out what might be done. Another meeting was set for the following Monday. Three people showed up.

And the Ducker Road Community Involvement Council was born. Cookie then began to go door to door at the homes where they knew drugs were being sold and used, telling the residents, "Stop, or we will stop you."

No sooner had they started their campaign than the threats on Cookie's life began. One drug dealer in particular sent him the message that he was affecting his livelihood, and the next time he saw Cookie, he would "blow his head off."

Cookie talked to his wife and told her that he was going over to the drug dealer's house to confront him. "I wasn't going to live my life in fear and always look over my shoulder," Cookie recalled.

"So I went to his house and knocked on the door and waited fifteen minutes for him to answer. When he finally came to the door, I said, 'Here I am. Go ahead and kill me. We are not going away, so if you want to blow my head off, do it now.'"

"You're crazy, man," he said and slammed the door. And that was it. The new message that the drug dealer was spreading around the neighborhood was a different one. Now he was telling everyone to "stay away from Cookie—he's crazy. All those years he spent climbing those poles and working on power lines has fried his brain."

Cookie knew that he and the council had to do more than just knock on doors to bring their neighborhood back to where it once was. So Cookie took his savings and bought three acres on Ducker Road. He let everyone know that there was a drug nuisance and abatement law on the books that stated if a house was known to be one where drug activity was being conducted, the law would confiscate the property.

The next step was Cookie and the council taking to the streets, taking pictures of the drug deals as they were happening, photographing the license plates of the cars as they came into the neighborhood, and delivering them to the houses of the dealers.

Within eight months, one by one the drug dealers left and, with them, their customers as well. The drugs might have been gone from the Ducker Street community, but there still was a lot of work to do.

Cookie then asked some of his friends to join him one Saturday to begin cleaning up his neighborhood. More than a dozen of Cookie's friends came out with the residents and began picking up trash, dismantling rusted play sets that hadn't been used for years, and helping transform Ducker Road to the community it had been so many years ago.

The efforts are far from over. Cookie receives calls at all hours of the day and night from families and individuals in his community who have nowhere else to turn. Cookie's days are now filled helping to provide housing, jobs, and food and providing Christmas gifts to nearly one hundred children a year. Cookie continues to assist young single mothers in finding their way to a better life for themselves and their children, as well as his anti-drug message that he brings to the Ducker Road community and to the young people and schools in our area.

He helps fund his outreach by growing and selling Japanese maples and holding his annual block party and anti-drug walk. He now owns nine properties that he rents to families who may not be able to find a home due to bad credit or a past record. Cookie's named his company

I Can Cove Properties, noting that it is not only a positive message but that the last four letters of *African* and *American* is "ican."

Cookie and his wife, Dianna, have two sons, eight grandchildren, and one great-grandchild. "But I have fifty-one children in our community who call me Granddaddy," he told me with a wide grin and a laugh.

"I have a real problem," he shared with me one day. "I just want to help people."

We would all be so much better if all of us shared the same problem as Cookie has.

And he proved that Muhammad Ali was correct; impossible is nothing.

Anyone who is familiar with Cookie's story has little doubt that he didn't fall prey to what so many of us do—spending more time discussing issues, convening committees, and assembling task forces to study the issues at hand and the problems that we face.

As well intentioned as all this may be, in many cases it does little to help those we strive to serve. It is easier to talk and strategize than it is to roll up our sleeves and get our hands dirty. In so many cases, those who call for assistance cannot wait for us to come up with the great plans and big answers to what they need now.

Studies certainly have their place but not when it interferes with those who are hurting, sick, alone, and frightened.

I can't believe that anyone whose heart is in making sure that we all do everything for those in need wants to be bogged down by studying a problem we already know exists, but it happens to us all the same.

It is good to remember the quote from G. K. Chesterton, in which he says, tongue in cheek, "I have searched all the parks in all the cities and found no statues of committees."

Mother Teresa would often say, "There should be less talk; a preaching point is not a meeting point. What do you do then? Take a broom and clean someone's house. That says enough."

Earlier on, we looked at the questions: How do we start? When we do begin? How do we know what to do?

Mother Teresa was asked the question of how she could act so quickly and so simply in addressing needs. In the book *Call to Mercy*, an Indian government official recounted that he would often ask Mother Teresa, "How would you know what to do? Let's say, there was a cyclone or a fire; how do you know what to do?"

She would answer, "We go and start the work. Everyone joins us. Everyone gives help, and then the work gets done."

The government official went on to say, "On one level she makes it sound very simple. On another level I think she came to realize that she and her sisters stood for a kind of dispassionate goodness that attracted the goodness of ordinary human beings—and we all have goodness in us—to join the effort, and the work gets done."

"We go and start the work ..."

Let us begin ...

Let Us Begin

- No matter what our vocation may be, we are all called to be kind and live a life of service to others.
- "Impossible" is not a fact. It is an opinion, a dare, a potential.
- Don't take too long in studying a problem or garnering information or putting together a committee. The longer you wait, the more will hurt. Go and start your work. Others will come.
- Kindness is something that everyone—no matter who they are or what their situation may be—can see, hear, and feel.

Chapter 10

THE POWER OF GRATITUDE

Keep your eyes open to your mercies. The man who
forgets to be thankful has fallen asleep in life.
—Robert Louis Stevenson

There is one piece to finding our callings or, even more important, allowing our callings to find us that many times seems to be absent from many conversations. And that piece is finding and exhibiting a sense of gratitude.

That is not just saying or having an attitude of a casual thank-you but having a deep, heartfelt gratefulness for where we are and what we are able to do for those we come into contact with and the situations we find ourselves in every day.

Most people are probably at least a bit familiar with Albert Einstein, his accomplishments, or the connotation that his name is synonymous with genius and a great intellect—even to the point that if you type in "Albert" on Google search, his name is the first one that comes up, sixty years after his death.

Born in 1879 in the kingdom of Wurttemberg in the German Empire, Dr. Albert Einstein was a theoretical physicist who developed the theory of relativity, which is one of the two pillars of modern physics. Known for his dozens of scientific theories and applications,

Einstein was known for his brilliance but there was far more to the man, historically known as the father of modern physics.

Being in Germany during the rise of Adolf Hitler and the National Socialist Party in the 1930s, Professor Einstein, along with his other Jewish colleagues, were forbidden by the new laws passed by the fascist government from holding any official positions, including teaching at universities.

In May 1933 his name was listed in a German magazine among those "not yet hanged." With a five-thousand-dollar bounty on his head, Dr. Einstein fled his native land and sought refuge in Belgium, London, and eventually the United States. It was his work that helped the Allies win the Second World War and stopped the onslaught of the German and Japanese forces. But he never saw that as his true work, as he championed the American civil rights movement, among other world peace initiatives.

Even with his worldwide reputation and global following, where hundreds of thousands hung on his every word and thoughts, two of his many quotes still resonate six decades after his passing.

The first is "I speak to everyone in the same way, whether he is the garbage man or the president of the university." Think of that—a Nobel Prize winner, professor at Princeton University, a man who was courted by presidents, kings, and prime ministers saw and kindly treated everyone the same, no matter his or her station in life.

But I think it is the second one that turned his heart and can turn ours toward a lifelong path of gratitude. That one simply states, "There are only two ways to live your life. One is as though nothing is a miracle. The other is as though everything is a miracle."

If everything in our lives were mundane, it would only be natural for us to get used to living a life where nothing really mattered. Gratitude may well be hard to muster. Einstein did find something in his situation to be grateful for, even though he was forced from his country because of his Jewish heritage. He saw everything in his life as a miracle.

If we choose to do the same, the opportunity for our heartfelt gratitude can abound. Heartfelt is not just a hackneyed term; it means that gratitude is a memory and an action that comes from our hearts, not our minds.

Author Melody Beattie noted, "Gratitude unlocks the fullness of life. It turns what we have into enough, and more. It turns denial into acceptance, chaos into order, and confusion into clarity … It turns problems into gifts, failures into success, the unexpected into perfect timing, and mistakes into important events. Gratitude makes sense of our past, brings peace for today and creates a vision for tomorrow."

There is no better example I know of the power of gratitude and how it magnifies itself into reaching others than what I have learned from my friend Father Jason Sanderson.

Each year I have the wonderful opportunity to go to Waterloo, Iowa, to help present the Lou Thesz World Heavyweight Championship Award.

The award, considered the Nobel Peace Prize for the sport of wrestling, is presented annually by the National Wrestling Hall of Fame Dan Gable Museum and the Eblen Center for Social Enterprise of Eblen Charities.

The award is presented to an individual in the sport of wrestling who has taken the skills, courage, and mental toughness that are the essentials of the sport and applied those characteristics to the realm of public service, offering assistance to those in need throughout the world.

This honor is named in memory of the legendary wrestling champion Lou Thesz, who held the NWA world title six times in four decades and who, along with his wife, Charlie, have long been instrumental in the work of Eblen Charities.

In 2008 the award was presented to Father Jason Sanderson from New Hampshire for his outstanding work around the world in building and establishing schools and orphanages, especially on the continent of Africa.

But it was not only Jason's spirit and compassion that impressed me but the insight that he offered upon receiving the award, a thought that hasn't left me since that night in June.

For some time now I have been hearing the word "blessed" quite a bit.

I know that being blessed can mean divinely or supremely favored or fortunate. I hear "Have a blessed day" as much as I hear "Have a good day," and in asking how you are, the response I hear frequently is "I'm blessed."

I am not questioning the sincerity of these folks or the use of the word, but it is what Jason said about being blessed and the gratitude that was instilled in him that gave me—and everyone in attendance that evening in Waterloo—pause.

As Jason spoke of his work, he relayed a story about his asking his priest and mentor the question, "Why have I been so blessed in my life?" He was hoping to hear of some wonderful thing he might have done in the past that had curried God's favor.

The priest's answer not only surprised him but also left an indelible mark on his heart that encouraged him to do the things that have touched so many lives.

The answer the priest gave was this: "You are not blessed because of something you have done. You are blessed so you can do greater things." I had never heard of receiving blessings in that vein, but it made all the sense in the world.

We are not given gifts and opportunities necessarily as some reward that we are to keep to ourselves and sit back and revel in our accomplishments and good fortune.

We are to use them to do greater things in reaching out to improve the lives of others, and it is in that that our lives are made better, and we are truly blessed.

There is a realization that the things we have been given are not rewards because of some great thing we have done but are to be used as tools to help others. Talents, money, connections, and inspiration are not meant for ourselves. They are given to us to help others.

It is in our gratitude that the fire is ignited in us to continue to reach out, even more than what we have done. The more we do, the more gratitude we should find, and the more gratitude we find, the more we will be compelled to do. It is a cycle of unending kindness that would never reach its ultimate potential without the power of gratitude.

We don't have to look far to find what we need to fuel the fire of gratitude in our hearts. As said early on, we just have to look, widen our thoughts, focus, see things in a brighter light, and choose to see, as Dr. Einstein suggested, everything in our lives as a miracle.

Taking time to open our hearts and minds to the world around us and calling our consciousness to the fact that we can take another breath, or that someone just held a door for us, or that we found a parking place on a busy shopping day can easily instill a thankfulness in us that will move us to do more and share what we have been given.

It is important that you do not to keep your gratitude to yourself. Express it to those who have shown kindness to you and those to whom you have shown kindness. Let them know how much you appreciate what they have done for you or that you are grateful to have the opportunity to help them, and thank them for giving you the chance.

I think G. K. Chesterton said it best when he wrote, "I would maintain that thanks are the highest form of thought and that gratitude is happiness doubled by wonder."

It is the last part that stops me where I stand. I realize that there is another part of gratitude that I never really thought about, and that is if we see wonder in the happiness that comes from being thankful, it comes from a humble heart.

In that I mean that if we are grateful for the kind deeds that others bestow on us, we have at some point realized that we are not the center of the universe.

The kindness that has been shown to us has nothing to do with who we are. It is about who the person is who has done something selfless to make things better for us. It means that we have been paying attention to others in a different way. We are aware of what others are doing for us.

It's not because we deserve it but because someone cared about the situation we were in or what we may have needed at the time. That is why we are grateful; we may not think we deserve the benevolence shown to us, but we received it.

Folks who possess a spirit and mind-set of gratefulness notice the goodness and kind deeds that others do for them, no matter how small they may seem to others.

Those who don't possess such a spirit miss the actions done on their behalf because they believe that they deserve it, as they are so much better than anyone else. So of course they should receive all that is given to them and more.

People who are grateful are humble. They are thankful for what they have and for even the smallest kindness shown to them, and they find that inspires them to do the same for others.

They are aware that so much in life is fragile and that a day can easily bring difficult times as well as good things. They appreciate what others may forgo to reach out to help them and others.

Grateful people are sensitive to the fact that there are so many who are struggling and are less fortunate than they are. It is quite a paradox how it appears that those who are grateful for what they have seem to have more.

Those who do not hold an attitude of thankfulness only think of themselves and seldom notice what others may do for them or what they may have had to give up personally.

Sadly it seems that those who are not thankful for what they have are always looking for more and will never have enough.

At the National Prayer Breakfast held in Washington, DC, in 1994, Mother Teresa shared this story of the power that simple words of gratitude can have.

> One evening several of our sisters went out, and we picked up four people from the street. One of them was in a most terrible condition.
>
> So I told the other sisters, "You take care of the other three; I will take care of this one who looks the worst."
>
> So I did for the woman everything that my love could do. I cleaned her and put her in bed, and there was such a beautiful smile on her face.
>
> She took hold of my hands and said two words in her native language, Bengali: "Thank you." Then she died.

I could not help but examine my conscience and ask, "What would I say if I were in her place?"

My answer was simply that I would have tried to draw a little attention to myself.

I would have said, "I am hungry ... I am dying ... I am in pain."

But the woman gave me much more; she gave me grateful loving, dying with a grateful smile on her face.

It means that even those with nothing can give us the gift of thanks.

Another story from Mother Teresa's life shows that even when she was refused what she asked for on the behalf of others, she never lost the sense of gratitude.

Mother Teresa never hesitated to go out and beg for things that were needed for those she and her sisters served, whether it was clothing, food, medical supplies, water, medication, or any other things that might help ease the suffering of those who called out for help.

On one particular occasion, Mother Teresa was seeking medication for a little girl who was suffering from tuberculosis. She was going door to door, trying to find a physician who would extend her kindness and give her the medicine she needed to help alleviate the little girl's pain.

One doctor she approached was particularly arrogant and disrespectful in his refusal to grant Mother Teresa her request. After listening quietly to him, she got up from her chair, smiled at the physician, and simply said, "Thank you," and left his office to continue her search.

She hadn't reached the door to the street when someone from the doctor's office found her and asked her to come back to his office. When she reentered his office, the physician was quite puzzled on why Mother

Teresa had so graciously thanked him after he offered her nothing for the little girl.

Then he inquired what she might say if he handed her the medicine she was requesting. Mother Teresa responded that the first time she asked, the refusal was for her. Now, if he found it in his heart to give her the medication, she would gratefully accept it for the poor that she served.

The doctor, somewhat bewildered by Mother Teresa's kindness and gentleness toward him, handed her the medication for the little girl. The power of gratefulness in the face of refusal can at times turn even the hardest of hearts.

I am drawn to believe that Mother Teresa did not necessarily feel the gratitude she showed the doctor for his refusal to help this little girl but that it was more of thankfulness for the time he gave her and gratefulness for the opportunity that she had been given to serve this little girl in her time of need.

She saw a much bigger picture that God had painted. One or a dozen refusals didn't diminish the joy she had and the gratefulness that she had to be able to be part of seeking help on behalf of this little girl and so many others she had the great privilege to serve.

Sometimes gratitude can come from places and people that you would never expect, which is what makes it all the more powerful and why it reaches the deepest depths of our hearts.

One morning some time ago, I met a lady in our office who has not left my mind since I shook her hand. She was sitting alone in our lobby when I walked through; I went over to her and said good morning.

She nodded and replied, "Good morning. How are you?"

Her words came out very thick and hard to understand. At first I thought she might have a speech impediment, but impediment or not, it did not seem to interfere with her asking me how I was.

I told her I was fine and thanked her for asking. I offered her something to drink and asked how we could help her. She told me she had been in the day before and had come back to see one of our counselors who was helping her with her power bill and some other bills. I said we were glad that she came in and that someone would be right with her.

She explained that when she first came in, she wasn't expecting anyone to help her but thought she would come in and ask. She was surprised that we would offer her so much help and was grateful for the kindness that was shown to her.

She was in desperate need of her medication as well. As she explained her situation, the counselor said, "I am so sorry you are having to go through all of this."

She looked up, smiled, and said, "Why are you feeling sorry for me? The Lord has given me another day."

I overheard the conversation and thought, *What a remarkable attitude for someone who has come here for assistance.*

But in hearing her story, my appreciation turned into amazement.

This cheerful lady was more concerned with how everyone was in our office than she was for her own health.

Her speech wasn't thick and slowed because of a speech impediment but as a side effect of the medication she was taking.

She had eight surgeries in less than three months due to the cancer that had spread through her body, and she recently found out that her cancer had spread to her stomach, and she might not live until Christmas.

Facing her own death, her concern was for her family and the kindness she showed to us in the office.

We were able to help her with her electric bill and a number of other things that she needed immediately. Even though we were able to help with things that she could not receive help for elsewhere, we could not help her with what she was facing.

She was just so thankful for the fact that she had another day to be here with her family. She shared that happiness and outlook with all of us that day.

I am thankful to have had the honor to have met this wonderful lady and have always been mindful that we receive so much more from those we serve than they ever receive from us.

And I will be forever grateful that she reminded us all that we have another day and, again, the true heart of living a life of thankfulness.

Gratitude is not just an expression of thankfulness, but as this wonderful dying woman showed us, it's an attitude that we carry in our hearts every minute of every day. It is a simple mind-set that can quickly transform who we are and how we view the world around us.

It doesn't matter if we have ever followed that path before this day. All that matters is that we start now. If you don't believe that you have the heart, you don't have to look far to find it.

In 1976, Christian singer, songwriter, and the often-recognized "father of Christian rock," Larry Norman, released "I Am a Servant," and the words he wrote encapsulate where a life of service begins. In the final line of the song, he wrote, "To live's a privilege, to love is such an art."

They are simple words that bring the life of service for which we search into focus.

"To live's a privilege, to love is such an art" …

Let us begin …

Let Us Begin

- Very little of what we experience in life is more powerful than gratitude.
- We are not blessed because we have done something special or have found particular favor with God. We are blessed so we can do greater things.
- A spirit of gratitude opens us to notice acts of kindness that we may otherwise have missed.
- No matter if we have nothing to give; we all can still give the gift of thanks.
- Always be prepared to say thank you, even if you fall short of your goal or have not received things you have hoped.

Chapter 11

IN THE FINAL ANALYSIS

Give the world the best you have and it may never be enough:
Give the world the best you have anyway.
—Mother Teresa of Calcutta

On the wall of Shishu Bhavan, her children's home in Calcutta, Mother Teresa posted nine simple sentences that have been copied and shared countless times around the world. But in those sentences, Mother Teresa's enduring and poignant message presents the path to everyone who desires to serve.

Known as "In the Final Analysis," the words written provide not only the first steps to an unselfish life of service and meaning but also provide a constant reminder of what we need to keep in mind as we grow in and continue on with our lives of reaching out to others.

Originally written in 1968 as part of a student leadership manual for high school students, titled "The Silent Revolution," nineteen-year-old Harvard University sophomore Kent Keith wrote the "Paradoxical Commandments."

As the turbulent era of the 1960s was beginning to wane, it seemed a great part of the generation who was coming of age was striving to find their way through extremely difficult times.

Keith's message was unique for those times. He saw that the change that the new and younger generation sought in the world would have to come through selfless service, not through the defiance and self-centeredness that seemed to prevail.

He encouraged his students to look to change the world not by retaliating against the system but rather by working within the system by caring for others.

The reason was that he had seen so many who lost heart and became discouraged, seeing their high hopes and lofty ideals dashed after going into the world. Their thoughts, ideas, and works were shut out, ignored, or ridiculed.

He told them that if they truly wanted to make any type of lasting change to a turbulent and troubled world, they would have to find a deeper meaning to who they were and what they were trying to accomplish. That meaning would uphold them through difficulty, disappointment, and rejection.

Kent impressed upon them that if they really wanted to find meaning in their lives and actually give something of value back to the world, it would have to come from a dedication to serve because of the love they had, not just because it might be the fashion of the time.

It would be that which would sustain them in the face of opposition and ridicule. He went on to explain that if they were seeking recognition, they might only find disappointment. But if they did it only for the sake of doing what was right, if they did what was right, they would find meaning and satisfaction, and that in itself would be enough.

If what they did had meaning, they wouldn't need acclaim.

I am sure it is what British author, poet, educator, soldier, philologist, theologian, and creator of Middle Earth, J. R. R. Tolkien, meant when he wrote, "Deeds will not be less valiant because they are unpraised."

It was from this almost lost essay that some of the greatest guidance for a life of service and meaning in a troubled world could come.

Here is Dr. Keith's original Paradoxical Commandments:

People are illogical, unreasonable, and self-centered.
Love them anyway.

If you do good, people will accuse you of selfish ulterior motives.
Do good anyway.

If you are successful, you will win false friends and true enemies.
Succeed anyway.

The good you do today will be forgotten tomorrow.
Do good anyway.

Honesty and frankness make you vulnerable.
Be honest and frank anyway.

The biggest men and women with the biggest ideas can be shot down by the smallest men and women with the smallest minds.
Think big anyway.

People favor underdogs but follow only top dogs.
Fight for a few underdogs anyway.

What you spend years building may be destroyed overnight.
Build anyway.

People really need help but may attack you if you do help them.
Help people anyway.

Give the world the best you have and you'll get kicked in the teeth.
Give the world the best you have anyway.

It was from the Paradoxical Commandments that Mother Teresa's "In the Final Analysis" would emerge. But I believe that Dr. Keith's commandments were not given as advice but as a challenge.

The challenge is to always endeavor to do what is right, good, and true, even if no one values it. The challenge is to keep striving even in the face of what may seem to be insurmountable adversity. Otherwise, so many of the things that need to be accomplished in the world never would be accomplished.

That deep caring for others provides the motivation and gives the vision and strength to see what we need to do and to do it. If we are doing things only for our own sakes or for our own recognition, what we do can easily fail in the long run.

But if we do everything from the heart, no matter what is or is not accomplished, the love we put into our actions will echo throughout eternity.

Mother Teresa knew this and certainly must have seen it in Dr. Keith's writing as she took eight of his ten Paradoxical Commandments, added one of her own, and placed it on the wall in Calcutta.

As with so many things that Mother Teresa touched, the heart and the meaning of "In the Final Analysis" transcend mere words. She added her own touch to make even the most simple tasks or words more powerful and significant. Mother Teresa's "In the Final Analysis" has and continues to touch millions.

In the Final Analysis

People are often unreasonable, illogical, and self-centered; forgive them anyway.

If you are kind, People may accuse you of selfish, ulterior motives; be kind anyway.

If you are successful, you will win some false friends and some true enemies; succeed anyway.

If you are honest and frank, people may cheat you; be honest and frank anyway.

What you spend years building, someone could destroy overnight; build anyway.

If you find serenity and happiness, they may be jealous; be happy anyway.

The good you do today, people will often forget tomorrow; do good anyway.

Give the world the best you have, and it may never be enough; give the world the best you've got anyway.

You see, in the final analysis, it is between you and God; it was never between you and them anyway.

Certainly these are powerful words from one of the most powerful people who has ever walked the earth. But as we look at these words, we see where the power comes from. It doesn't derive itself from physical or political strength, nor does it come from great intellect, education, or wealth.

This power comes from the strength of kindness.

I had the opportunity to write at some length about the Paradoxical Commandments and "In the Final Analysis" in 2015 in my book *In the Final Analysis—Mother Teresa's Enduring Message to All Who Serve*, and I saw so much value in what Mother Teresa wrote for all of us who are setting out to find our own Calcutta.

So let's take a few of the nine stanzas that shine the brightest light on our quest to live a life of service and meaning.

"People are often unreasonable, illogical, and self-centered; forgive them anyway."

"In the Final Analysis" begins with the statement that people are unreasonable, illogical, and self-centered. There is no getting away from it or even finding a way around it. We all are unreasonable, illogical, and self-centered. No matter who we are, even the best of us can be pretty wearying at times.

We don't have to look very hard to see that are all stubborn, insensitive, thoughtless, unreasonable, egotistical, and self-centered. It is difficult for all of us at times to admit that we are that way, but it doesn't take long for us to spot it in others.

But there is hope that although we are adrift in a sea of selfishness, there is forgiveness.

I believe that true service and forgiveness goes hand in hand. The essence of who we are begins here. And we cannot truly serve unless we are willing to forgive.

It was Mother Teresa's compassion and her willingness to ignore the illogical and unreasonable behavior that was at the heart of her life and service. Forgiveness can change a heart and, in that, lead to kindness that may change a life. And if enough lives are changed, so goes the world.

Here is a story that illustrates the great forgiveness that Mother Teresa taught:

One night in the midst of winter, the sisters at the Missionaries of Charity in Armenia heard a loud noise in their house. Going down the stairs, they saw a man wearing a mask, breaking in the front door.

He quickly approached the sisters, seized one of them, and held a large knife to her throat.

"Give me all your dollars!" he screamed.

The sister answered, "We don't have any."

"Rubles, then!" he commanded.

"We don't have any rubles in the house either," the sister calmingly said.

In desperation, the intruder demanded, "Then pack up something for me to eat."

He removed the knife from the sister's throat, and she and the other nuns went into their small kitchen and packed spaghetti, bread, jam, and whatever else they happened to find for the young man.

They also carefully packed a set of utensils and some salt as well.

As soon as the food was packed, the man grabbed the package of food from the sisters and ran out.

He ran through the chapel, and before he reached the front door, he turned and cried, "Your God will never forgive me."

The sister he'd held at knifepoint responded, "Yes, He will, if you ask Him for forgiveness."

The intruder moved to leave and then said to the sisters who were trembling in the cold, "You must close the door behind me."

But the door would not close; he had damaged it while breaking in, so there was no way to keep the cold winter night winds out of the chapel.

When he saw how helpless the sisters were and how they were shivering in the cold, he asked them to bring him a hammer and some nails, and he began to fix the door he had broken.

As soon as he had fixed the damage he had done to the door, he grabbed the food the sisters had packed for him, closed the door, and ran off into the night.

Was it a life of service of the Missionaries of Charity that led to the forgiveness of the young man, or was it the kindness of the sisters that led to their forgiveness? Forgiveness can only strengthen kindness, and true kindness can only lead to our forgiving those who may have hurt us.

Forgiveness is where we start. Kindness is where we end.

Let us begin ...

Let Us Begin

- In your life of service, look for meaning, not recognition.
- Service and forgiveness go hand in hand. We cannot truly serve if we are unwilling to forgive.
- The act of forgiveness can change both the heart of the forgiven and the one who forgives.
- A change of heart can easily lead to many lives being changed, not just yours but all those around you as well.
- Forgiveness is where a life of service begins. Kindness is where it ends.

Chapter 12

DOING GOOD ANYWAY

No act of kindness, however small, is ever wasted.
—Aesop

In the last chapter we looked at Mother Teresa's "In the Final Analysis" and how its thoughts can help us in our path to a life of meaning and service. In this chapter we will look at a few more of the verses that illuminate the life of service and meaning we seek.

"If you are kind, people may accuse you of selfish, ulterior motives; be kind anyway."

It certainly is sad to think that so many folks tend to think that when someone does an act of kindness that they are doing it for some selfish motive. It is as if true kindness and altruism do not really exist, and what is claimed to be unselfish acts are only done for selfish reasons.

In the cruel light of distrust that exists toward any good works, why should we even bother to do anything for anyone? Why should we expend the effort, time, or expense to help someone who not only may not be grateful for it but will look at our actions with disregard and accuse us of everything but selfless motives?

If we are looking for recognition or praise, there absolutely is no reason to continue on this particular path. The odds of attaining these things are long, if we achieve them at all. If that is all we are seeking in our acts of kindness, it might be a good idea to take stock and reexamine our motives.

If you find that you are only doing this for your own glory or to gain anything in the process, it is probably better to stop now. You are only doing more harm than good to those you are being "kind" to and to yourself.

What little good that may be done will be just that—little good.

If the only incentive of a life of doing kind works is to gain the praise of those around us, in all probability it won't last for long, if we do gain it. It is easy to get disheartened and cynical if we are only doing the guise of good works to shine the light on ourselves. The heart of our kindness will easily go out of our work if there was little or no heart in it in the beginning.

But there is also a great number of people who don't think that being kind to someone or helping someone in need is doing anything extraordinary or out of the ordinary. They don't have to give the situation any thought or take time to think about it or pray about it.

They already know the answer, and the answer is yes.

They don't stop to wonder what others may think their motives are, nor do they talk about what they have done or whom they might have helped; there is nothing to tell, as far as they are concerned.

There is a chance that any time we reach out to help anyone in need, there will be those who do all they can to criticize and attack us.

Mother Teresa had detractors as well, and some of them were relentless in their criticism of her and her work.

She endured political attacks from within and outside of India because she would not take a specific stand on Indian governmental affairs and the fact that she would not use her influence to change the power structure or politics of India or any other country. She was also accused of only trying to promote herself and her own political agenda.

None of this mattered to Mother Teresa, and it did not divert or dissuade her from what she was called to do. She didn't stop to question the veracity of those who chose to assail her. She loved them as she loved those who were less fortunate that she was serving.

Her calling, as it is ours, was not to just love those she was serving but everyone, whether they loved her or not.

If we are called to be kind to others, we should not be dissuaded by what people think and say that our reasons are. If our only motive is just to be kind and reach out to those in need, what does it matter what others think?

In the early days of her ministry Mother Teresa came upon a man lying on a sidewalk near death. She took him to the closest hospital, which refused to admit him, telling her that he would die whether they admitted him or not.

The hospital turned Mother Teresa and this dying man back out on the street. She left the man as she went to a pharmacy to get some medicine to help ease his suffering. When she returned, she found the man had died. Died in the gutter, died in the dust of Calcutta, died alone. Mother Teresa knew that she must do something to make sure it didn't happen again.

"Then the idea occurred to me of creating a home where dying people could finish out their lives, where someone would help them, where they would see a face of a person next to them who would smile lovingly and help them understand they shouldn't be afraid because they were going to their Father's house," Mother Teresa recalled.

Mother Teresa approached city officials and asked them, "Give me at least a room," and the officials agreed to let her have the temporary use of a vacant building that had been used as a place to rest for pilgrims next to the temple of the goddess Kali. She named it Nirmal Hriday, which is Bengali for "The Place of the Immaculate Heart."

Nirmal Hriday was set up on the site of the holy Temple of Kalighat that housed four hundred Hindu priests. Many who were against Mother Teresa and her work accused her of being there only to convert the people to Christianity, not to care for the dying, as she claimed. There were numerous lawsuits and constant attacks questioning Mother Teresa's sincerity.

One influential Indian official vowed publicly that he would personally see that the Missionaries of Charity were removed from the temple at all costs.

He visited Nirmal Hriday while building his case against Mother Teresa and collecting complaints against her. As a crowd of his supporters waited outside, he walked through the aisles, surrounded by those his city and his country had forsaken. He saw firsthand how the sisters cared for those whose lives were slipping away.

Seeing the love and devotion that Mother Teresa and her sisters expressed in caring for those who were dying moved him. He saw the compassion of Mother Teresa and the Missionaries of Charity as they served the poorest of the poor facing the end of their lives.

They reached and loved the ones that his society had cast aside as they washed the wounds and fed those in their care. When he left the home of the dying, he spoke to the crowd who was waiting for him outside.

"I promised to throw the sisters out of here, and I will do it but only when you bring your mothers, wives, sisters, and daughters to do the work they are doing. You have a goddess of stone in the temple; here you have a living goddess."

Not long after this, one of the priests from the temple of the goddess Kali was stricken with tuberculosis, which is greatly feared throughout India. Even though the priests of Kali were at the forefront of those working to oust Mother Teresa and her sisters from their grounds, Mother Teresa took in the highly contagious priest and took care of him as he was racked with fever.

Each day, his fellow priests would visit him and see how kindly he and the others were being cared for and how selflessly the sisters put themselves at risk of catching the disease themselves. One by one, the priests reached out to Mother Teresa and became her most ardent supporters.

Mother Teresa showed great kindness to the very people who set out to stop her and was the first to come to their aid when they needed help the most. She didn't bear a grudge or seek retribution by withholding the assistance or turning her head, pretending not to see. She quickly opened the doors to care for those who harbored nothing but ill toward her. Her kindness turned their hatred into admiration and support.

"If you are kind, people may accuse you of selfish, ulterior motives; be kind anyway …"

Ralph Waldo Emerson wrote, "You cannot do a kindness too soon, for you never know how soon it will be too late." In this, he is reminding us that there are only so many tomorrows, and every chance we miss in helping those in need is an opportunity we may never have again. And by our hesitance or just refusal to help, those who may so desperately need our help will continue to suffer and feel alone.

Mother Teresa recounted the following story, which all too sadly exemplifies what the poet had penned so many years before.

"Some time ago a woman came with her child to me and said 'Mother, I went to two or three places to beg for food for we have not eaten for three days but they told me that I was young, and I must work and eat. No one gave me anything.' I went to get some food and by the time I returned, the baby in her hand had died of hunger. I hope it was not our convents that refused her."

A simple act of kindness would have easily saved this baby's life. It was a simple act of kindness that was refused and in its wake, untold sorrow.

We all have so much kindness in our hands that we can freely give to others, but so many times our personal feelings and philosophies get in the way because we believe we have to follow our own beliefs.

And as we all know, our personal beliefs can never be wrong, can they?

In the case of the young mother that Mother Teresa spoke of, the personal philosophies of the ones she begged food from may have made them believe they were righteous, but the consequences of their rectitude allowed a baby to die of hunger and its mother to grieve for the rest of her life.

Mother Teresa wrote in "In the Final Analysis," "The good you do today, people will often forget tomorrow; do good anyway."

She also would often remind those who wished to follow her example by saying, "We only have today." Tomorrow only exists in the abstract, and for those who are hurting, tomorrow is an eternity away, and the todays are long and often without hope.

I believe that Mother Teresa's words in this particular paradoxical commandment have as much to do about the "today" as they do about the good we do being forgotten. How many times have we pretended we didn't see someone in need, or we thought to ourselves, *It's already late. I'll check on them tomorrow*, or *They live all the way across town; it can wait until tomorrow*—only to wish we had acted sooner. We lament with a broken heart, "If only I had called them last night," or "If only I had taken a few extra minutes to let them know they weren't alone." If only ...

Not all of Mother Teresa's endeavors were successful. Many times it seemed that all the good she had done was forgotten, as she and her Missionaries of Charity were not welcome in many places that they visited.

Mother Teresa and four of her sisters traveled to the war-torn city of Belfast in 1972 hoping to serve those in need and to help bring peace to the Catholic–Protestant conflict that had injured and killed so many. Mother Teresa believed that her joining with a group of Anglican nuns would help bridge the gap of the sectarian violence as they served those who were injured by the violence in their streets.

But she was far from welcome and was all but forced out of the city. She encountered the same reaction as she went to Sri Lanka when all foreign religious orders were expelled from the country.

But her work was not about being remembered but about reaching those who are in need of help. She looked at these incidents not as failures but as opportunities for God to lead her to where He wanted her to go.

She would do good anyway, regardless of what the reaction to her and her order might be.

Another lesson that we must all learn from Mother Teresa is that she knew very well the difference between motion and action. She continually stressed that talking about serving and actually serving are far from being the same thing.

"If you are preoccupied with people who are talking about the poor, you scarcely have time to talk to the poor. Some people talk about hunger but they don't come and say 'Mother, here is five Rupees; buy food for these people.' But they can give a beautiful lecture on hunger."

Talking excessively, endless meetings, and conferences are luxuries that those we serve cannot afford.

Hunger, sickness, eviction, and loneliness have no heart and will not wait. While so many of us talk about how to win the war, those on the front line are losing battles every day. We use up today talking about tomorrow.

Mother Teresa had been known to say, "Don't wait for leaders. Do it yourself, person to person." While others may have met over breakfast or lunch to discuss the hunger of those outside their doors, Mother Teresa and her sisters were prepared to do what was necessary to feed those who were hungry that morning.

There is no better example of service to all of us who want to reach those who are less fortunate, and the salient question is how far are we willing to go to help someone in need of our help? Whether or not it is forgotten does not matter.

At the end of "In the Final Analysis," Mother Teresa gives us the most significant advice for anyone who searches for a life of meaning and seeks a life of service to others. In a mere twenty-one words she says it all.

"Give the world the best you have, and it may never be enough; give the world the best you have anyway."

In the Gospel of Saint Luke is the well-known story of the widow's mite, in which a woman of meager means gave all she had to help others. She did so quietly and, I can imagine, with her head down and with a grateful heart.

Luke recalled Jesus's words that this poor widow gave much more than all the rich who went before her to give to the temple's treasury and who made sure that everyone there was aware of their "generosity."

He explained that the reason was that they gave out of their abundance, while she gave out of her poverty. She sacrificed food or something else she truly needed while the wealthy who gave did so out of what they did not need.

The coin itself was actually called a *lepta* and was worth about six minutes of work, and it was all she had. She was giving the world the best she could give.

By worldly standards it was not much. In the eyes of the world, that unimportant sum could never make any difference to anyone.

But God sees things differently. As He said to Samuel, "For God sees not as man sees, for man looks at the outward appearance, but the Lord looks at the heart." (I Samuel 16:7)

And that is what giving the best you have is all about.

Giving the world the best you have, by worldly standards, will probably never be enough for a world that continues to crave and demand more. But giving the best you have is not about pleasing the world or meeting its requirements or expectations.

It is simply about giving your best because it is your best. It is what you wish to give others; it is what you offer to God. Never enough, I suppose, depends on whom you ask.

Mother Teresa shared this story that echoes what Jesus taught about the widow's mite. One evening around sunset, Mother Teresa heard a knock on her door. Answering it, she found, as she said, "Jesus in the shape of a poor leper," shivering from the cold and who obviously had nothing to eat for many days.

She quickly arranged for the man to have some food and a blanket to cover him. The leper looked at her and said with the deepest sincerity, "Mother, I have not come here today to get anything for myself. I have heard people say that you have received a big prize from somewhere. So I too decided this morning that I would offer you as a present the entire alms that I received today. I begged today from morning until this time, and whatever I have gotten is in this alms plate. Mother, kindly accept my humble present for your poor."

He reached out his hand, holding the alms plate that held all that he possessed in the world. Mother Teresa hesitated, knowing that this man was giving everything he had, and in doing so he very well might not have anything to eat for a number of days. But seeing how important that the gift was to this kind and humble man, she gratefully accepted the gift.

In the plate was seventy-five *paise* (a little less than a dollar). Mother Teresa kept those coins on her table. She spoke of this often and how this gift continually reminded her of how generous those in need could be.

This wonderful man showed that the best you have does not have to be on a large scale. The best you have comes from your heart. It may be small by the standard of the world or the times in which we live; but in giving and serving, those standards really don't matter.

It seems every time you turn on television or radio or pick up a newspaper or magazine you hear or read the words universal, global, international, or a number of other words that lean toward something big. Seemingly almost everyone wants to be part of something big, and that "big" is so much more important than something small.

With a "the bigger the better" attitude, it is not difficult to lose sight of the importance of things that many consider unimportant. But it is within those small things that great love and importance is hidden.

Mother Teresa is known around the world for what she considered her "humble work." She was brought onto the world stage for working in the gutters in service of the poorest of the poor. She, above all, knew the importance of things that others considered small. She showed us all what great things happen when small things are done.

"We must not drift away from humble works because these are works nobody will do. They are never too small. We are so small we look at things in a small way. Even if we do a small thing for somebody, God, being almighty, sees everything as great. For there are many people who can do big things, but there are very few people who will do the small things," Mother Teresa reminds us.

And it is in those "small things" we find true service. It is in those "small things" that we find the meaning in our lives that we have been looking for. It is in those "small things" that we so often give the world the best we have.

Acts of kindness never have to be done on a large scale. If the best you have today is opening a door for someone, helping him carry his groceries to his car, taking a moment to sit and listen or share a smile, these acts alone will resonate through the lives of those around us and make the world a so-much-better place.

Give the world the best you have, and it may never be enough; give the world the best you have anyway ...

Let us begin...

Let Us Begin

- No act of kindness is ever wasted, no matter how small you think it is.
- Recognition for our good deeds should never be the reason for our kindness toward others.
- Don't listen to those who criticize you for doing good. They will always be there. Remember that what you are called to do has nothing to do with them anyway.
- As difficult as it may be, show great kindness to everyone, especially to those who curse and attack you.
- Even though the good you do may quickly be forgotten by everyone, continue to do good always. Your kindness is much stronger and will resonate much longer than anyone's memory.

Chapter 13

THE CALCUTTA AROUND US

The best way to find yourself is to lose
yourself in the service of others.
—Mahatma Gandhi

When you are hungry, nothing else matters. These seven words have defined an amazing journey and outreach that has provided more than 500,000 meals to children in western North Carolina and millions of meals around the country in a little more than three years.

This story and the impact it has had for hundreds of thousands of children began as what restaurant entrepreneur and Arby's franchisee Joe Brumit considered a near calamity that nearly took the business he and his wife, Janice, had built during two previous decades.

"Mistakes can help you become who you are," Joe recalled as we were talking one afternoon at lunch at Juicy Lucy's. "I do believe that so much of what has brought me here today was for me and my company to be able to come back and help create these programs that help ensure that no child in our community has to face hunger while away from school."

The programs Joe was referring to are the Arby's / Eblen Charities JoyFULL Holidays at Home, Headlock on Hunger, Hoops Against

Hunger, and Huddle Against Hunger, all of which partner with the wrestling, basketball, and football communities, respectively.

But all of this is a long way from where Joe and Janice planned to be as they sold their business and looked to retirement and is even further from where Joe began his incredible story.

Long before Joe built the successful Brumit Restaurant Group and long before he walked to the forefront to lead the fight against childhood hunger, he and his family were making their way, as were so many others, in eastern Tennessee.

Born in Johnson City, Tennessee, Joe was the middle child and only son born to Joe and Gerry Brumit. When he was eight years old, Joe and Gerry moved with their two daughters and son to Oak Ridge, Tennessee, where Joe, Sr. began work as a machinist for Union Carbide.

Living on the income of a machinist left the family of five with only enough for life's necessities.

"We never had an allowance," Joe remembers, "but every Sunday in church my mother and father would always make sure all of us had something to put into the collection plate. I learned early on how important it was to give, no matter how little it may seem, and how important it was to give from need and not from what we might have as extra. It is a lesson I have always been grateful for and have never forgotten."

By his own admission, Joe excelled more at football than academics and was never much more than a C student in high school. Even so, he was accepted into the business administration program at the University of Tennessee, with designs of becoming an accountant.

Deciding not to return after his freshman year, Joe married and continued his job at Burger Chef to support himself and his new wife as she finished her degree.

He continued the career that would ultimately take him to a place where he would feed tens of thousands of children each year as a store manager at Burger Chef in the small town of Alcoa, Tennessee.

That is where Joe met Janice Watson, a buyer for JCPenney. Being divorced for some time, one of Joe's employees mentioned that she knew someone he should meet, and three months later they were married; they have been together for almost forty years.

After eleven years with Burger Chef, Joe was offered a management position and a greater chance for advancement with Burger King in Knoxville and then on to Greensboro, North Carolina.

After moving to Atlanta with Burger King, three years later Joe was recruited by Hardee's where he oversaw six hundred stores. It was there where a phone call one morning would lead Joe to where his deepest heart's desire would meet the world's greatest need.

From his early days in the restaurant business, Joe had wanted to have the opportunity to own and operate his own franchise. Knowing this, a franchisee he had worked with at Burger King called him and asked him if he would be interested in joining him and becoming an operating partner of thirteen Arby's in western North Carolina.

Jumping at the chance, Joe and Janice moved to Asheville. In six years they had added Checkers Hamburgers to their holdings. Ultimately.,they split the Arby's and Checkers holdings and bought out their partner. Joe and Janice kept the Arby's restaurants as their part of the deal, and their partner kept the Checkers.

Taking a new business partner in 1995 to accelerate growth, the company and partnership prospered for more than a decade, and a few days before Christmas 2007, Joe received a surprise offer.

His business partner of the past dozen years offered to buy him out and take over the entire enterprise. After some consideration and a great deal of financial analysis, Joe and Janice agreed to sell their part of the company to their partner.

After a few months of legal and financial structuring, the deal was done, and Joe and Janice began looking forward to the next chapter of their lives. Or so they thought.

At first all was well, but after the first year it was clear that restructuring of the deal had to happen. By the end of the second year of the deal, things continued to get worse, and it was obvious that things needed to be unwound.

With conversations going nowhere, Joe was concerned that his former partner would file bankruptcy, leaving hundreds of employees without a job and no way to support their families. Joe saw what he and Janice had worked so hard to build being destroyed and sinking them deeply into debt.

So in a period of a little more than two years, Joe had little recourse other than to take back what had once been a thriving business, now in freefall. The plans he and Janice had would now have to put on a shelf.

When he took back the stores in 2009, sales had fallen 20 percent, and the income he had worked to build declined by 80 percent, with no end in sight.

There were more sleepless nights than Joe could remember as he worked relentlessly, along with his team, to save their company and the livelihoods of hundreds of employees who depended on him.

"I was really struggling with next steps," Joe remembers. "One Sunday morning while singing in the choir, my mind was far from the hymns we were singing. I was more worried than I had ever been. My mind kept racing on what my next move should be when I felt this peace come over me as I realized that this wasn't my problem; it was God's. And all of a sudden the weight of the world was lifted off my shoulders.

"Suddenly I was able to focus on what we needed to do to get people back in our stores and not just what we needed to do to survive. At the time, unemployment was at 10 percent, which meant 90 percent of our community was working. It was a new attitude that was now to prevail throughout our company and one that, along with some innovative menu changes by the brand, would bring us back and propel us forward."

But this is not a story of a rise, fall, only to rise again. This is not just a story of a tireless effort to save a company that he'd left in another's hand to see it nearly destroyed. Nor is it just a story of great business acumen.

This is not where Joe's story ends. It is where Joe's story begins. This is what brought Joe to find his own Calcutta.

"I was allowed to pull things back together for a reason."

It started with a simple and sad story. This little girl was only in middle school, but she knew all too well what no child at her age, or any age, should know.

She was hungry and had been hungry for some time. Not the hunger that boys and girls have between meals, but the hunger that comes from an empty table; this is the hunger that comes from not having enough food at home.

This brave young lady sat in her counselor's office and ate corn meal from a box that came in a backpack of food she was to take home. She had not eaten much while school was out on break, and she couldn't wait until she got home to eat. She opened the box and ate the corn meal out of her hand.

This didn't happen in a third-world country or in the most rural parts or the inner city of our country. It happened where we live in Buncombe County. But it doesn't happen just here; it is happening all around our country.

As one in five children in our nation struggle with hunger each day, many times the meals they receive at school are the only food they will have to eat, and when the holidays arrive, they face the chance of going hungry until they are back in class.

This is where Joe Brumit found his Calcutta.

As in many communities, we have a number of groups that help provide backpack programs that send food home from school with students for the weekend, but none that look to the longer breaks for Thanksgiving, Christmas, Easter, and summer.

"We were fortunate to have so many well-intentioned groups that would help provide food for two days of the weekend, but none that provided food for the week, two weeks, or the two months the students were out for the summer," tells Joe. "There was a bigger need to address and fill. The backpack programs were a great start, but we knew that children were hungry at home during the holidays. But to truly make a difference in childhood hunger in our community, we had to break the rules."

To reach out to these children, Joe, along with his Arby's team, the Brumit Restaurant Group, the Arby's Foundation, and Eblen Charities joined together to create Arby's JoyFULL Holidays at Home program.

Through our local school systems, students receive an Arby's meal card that they can present at any Arby's in our area each day and eat for free.

In addition to the Arby's meal cards, the program works hand in hand with the Ingles Markets Food for Thought program, and together they helped create Headlock on Hunger, Hoops Against Hunger, and Huddle Against Hunger, which work with the wrestling, basketball, and football teams, collecting food that is given to students as they leave for the holidays.

Since its inception, more than 500,000 meals have been provided in western North Carolina and the JoyFull Holidays at Home program has become a national outreach for the Arby's Foundation, providing hundreds of thousands of meals each year across the country.

In 2016 Joe and Janice, along with the Brumit Restaurant Group, were awarded the Arby's Global Franchisee of the Year.

Joe states simply, "We wanted to make sure that children in our own community have enough to eat, especially during those longer holiday breaks. We firmly believe that it is everyone's responsibility to reach out to these children."

When you are hungry, nothing else matters.

Just a few miles down the road from the Brumit Restaurant Group is another amazing couple whose story of finding a life of service and meaning came in a most unexpected way.

There is something about the word "home" that resonates like few others. For many of us, home is where we are comfortable; home is where our fondest memories reside, and home is where we belong.

One of the sadder moments of life is when people are forced by circumstances to have to leave their homes for some type of facility because there may be something they can no longer do on their own.

Many times, it may just be making sure that they turn off the oven, close the front door, take their medication, or any number of simple things that we all may take for granted but that would threaten their safety and peace of mind of their family and friends.

As simple as those things may be to most of us, these are monumental things that can test the ability of those facing new challenges to remain independent.

That was by far the case for tens of thousands of wonderful and courageous people, along with those who loved and cared for them.

That was, until Allen and Drue Ray found their own Calcutta and in that created a unique and affordable way for them to stay at home.

As we have seen with scores of those who have found their calling, their journey to Calcutta began what seemed light-years away.

Allen and Drue met while attending the University of Alabama at Birmingham. Allen was studying engineering, while Drue was studying occupational therapy and education.

The night they met, Allen was traveling back from a beach trip and called the head of work study from a pay phone to see if there were any openings to work the late class registration. He was assigned the A-B line, but as his good fortune would have it, Allen was moved to the C-F line, as a young lady named Drue Coates walked up to the table to register.

He was drawn quickly "to the only girl wearing a skirt" that morning. They began dating shortly thereafter and married in 1977. Transferring to the University of Alabama in Tuscaloosa. Allen finished with an engineering degree in metallurgy, and Drue completed her elementary/early childhood education degree.

Drue found a job teaching second grade, and Allen went to work as an engineer. But as happy as they were and as satisfying as their careers had quickly become, they both looked for more and to find the places where they were needed most.

It was their parents who instilled in them, early on, the importance of giving. And this had impressed on them the obligation they had to others.

"I was told early on what Anglican cleric and theologian John Wesley said, 'Do all the good you can. By all the means you can. In all the ways you can. In all the places you can. At all the times you can. To all the people you can. As long as ever you can.' And that was how we learned to see the world," Drue recalls. "I was raised Methodist, and this was indeed how I saw—and to a large degree, still see—the world."

She also saw what service and compassion could do in others' lives, as she had cousins with disabilities and learned in those young years to understand and not to be afraid of them, like some others her age were.

Allen shared the same heart as Drue, and even before they met, he looked to where he was needed most, becoming the youngest scout master in the nation at the age of twenty-one. On his twenty-first birthday, he took over an inner-city scout troop in Birmingham. He was actively involved in scout troops for thirty years and created a Boy Scout troop in Houston and a Cub Scout pack in Asheville (Allen still volunteers with Troop Eight in Asheville to this day).

While working as an engineer, he also found a talent for working with companies that were in trouble operationally and financially and turning them around. A friend asked him for some help in rescuing his small business. That grew into an opportunity that would set them on a road that would bring untold families a peace and freedom they may not have had without Allen and Drue.

In 1989 Allen and Drue created a nonprofit company, the purpose and mission of which was to make a difference in long-term care for people who were aging or had different abilities. During the years, it grew to fifteen companies in eight states. When their expected standards of care and supports were unmet by management companies, they did not hesitate to take over the management and day-to-day operations.

"It was a leap of faith. It certainly was the right thing to do," Allen said. "We had no idea what this was going to be or how we were going to do it. All we knew is that we were making a commitment to those who had a lesser voice, if they had any voice at all."

They began by installing air conditioners and renovating the bathrooms, as some facilities were not far removed from "hosing down" their residents in large shower rooms once a week. Allen and Drue believed many people in those homes could, with a little help, be living on their own instead of being warehoused in a place they did not see as their home.

As the role of Medicaid and how it reimbursed their providers was ever changing, a prominent provider said to Allen that they should take advantage of Medicaid and "get all they could" while they could, before it changed.

With those statements he saw that the provider was far more concerned about the dollars than those being served. Understanding there was no compromise, Allen and Drue knew it was time to move on and create something else.

So they walked away from more than 100 million dollars in assets and transitioned the company and its thousands of employees to other nonprofit providers. But the question remained: move on to what?

But at the time, changing the continuum of care was just an idea—an idea without an impetus—but that wouldn't last for long, as the world of Medicaid and insurance reimbursement would change. The difference of philosophy would turn this idea into a life-changing reality for thousands of those in need.

"We had no intention of starting a new company," Drue said, "but it was time to try something new. We couldn't just place people where there was a bed available but where they would like to live and where it would be best."

With no clear path ahead, Allen and Drue visited a friend in Charleston, South Carolina, who had a company that provided and installed technology for Smart Homes. Their friend showed them his products and services, including things such as a small television installed in the corner of the bathroom mirror, home theaters, and lighting controls.

As innovative as his products were, Allen's and Drue's hearts were still with those who were being sent to care facilities where they didn't belong. As they were leaving, their friend said, "Hold on; I have one more thing to show you."

Walking back into his showroom, the friend shared a story about a customer who was an emergency room surgeon who was raising his sixteen-year-old son. Because the doctor was away from home quite a bit, he was concerned that his son and his friends were helping themselves to his liquor cabinet. He wanted to find a way to know what was happening in his absence so he could be an informed parent.

Their friend repurposed a sensor that was placed on the inside of the door so that every time it was opened, the doctor would receive a message on his pager. Problem solved by technology.

On their way home, Drue and Allen started talking; they had very little interest in providing Smart Homes with all the bells and whistles, but what if they could use the sensor technology to help those with disabilities who were living in an institution but could be living independently? What if staff or family could be alerted when an outside door was left open, the stove wasn't turned off, or any other thing that might be construed as a hazard?

And so, SimplyHome was born.

The idea behind this new mission was as straightforward as its name. They would develop technology and work with individuals who might be living with mental and physical challenges and, with supporting agencies, families, and service providers, enable those individuals to remain in their own homes instead of being institutionalized.

Through their innovative supports, paid staff, family members, neighbors, church members, and friends could be a part of the new outcomes created in a place called home.

"We began looking for the barriers keeping people from living on their own. Each person's challenges are different, and we wanted to work to create solutions for them and to overcome those impediments," Allen remembered from those early days.

It wasn't long before Allen and Drue got their chance to see if the idea of SimplyHome would work. In 2004, the state of Wisconsin was preparing to close a number of institutional care facilities. Group homes, adult family homes, and community-based residential facilities were to replace institutions. These programs, while smaller, would still be staffed and would provide a most supportive living environment for many of those who were affected.

Allen approached state officials with their new idea of providing technology to support the 154 individuals who were being displaced. The goal was to assist these individuals in living in a smaller community or in their own homes or apartments instead of placing them somewhere only because a bed was available.

Although officials were resistant at first, Allen believed that what they had to offer would be life-changing for the 154 families who were facing heart-wrenching uncertainty, but it also would save the state millions of dollars in the coming years.

With the support of one Wisconsin county funding agency in Brown County, Allen went straight to the families.

As the families agreed to provide guarded support, the funder's willingness to move individuals into a more independent setting, staff ready to meet the challenges, and sensors ready, 154 very excited people with disabilities moved into their own homes.

The use of SimplyHome technology, paired with necessary but greatly reduced staff support, allowed them to remain in their own homes.

More than a decade later, these folks are still living happily and successfully in these wonderful communities, where their lives are so much better than they would have been in the sterile institutions that awaited so many of them. Not only that, each year those living in the community and their families get together for a large picnic, celebrating the opportunity they have and the lives they continue to lead, thanks to the bringing together of staff support, assistive technology, and the support of family, friends, and neighbors.

As SimplyHome's assistive technology grew, Allen and Drue became consultants to the popular television show on ABC, *Extreme Makeover—Home Edition*. SimplyHome's role was to provide their technology in the home makeovers that would allow as much independence as possible to the individual who was dealing with physical challenges, which otherwise would preclude him or her from living at home.

They installed pressure pads that alerted caregivers when their family member got out of bed, voice-activated medication dispensers, blood pressure and heart rate monitors, and sensors that were activated when the stove had been on too long, a door was left open, or there was no movement in the home during a certain period of time. All alerts were sent to a family member or caregiver by electronic notification on their smartphones, tablets, or other devices.

One of Allen's favorite stories from one of the shows was after they fitted the home he asked the young man, "If you could change something here to make things better for you, what would it be?"

The young man, a quadriplegic, answered that he would very much like a way to talk on the phone with his girlfriend without his mother or father having to hold the phone up to his ear.

So Allen and his team went quickly back to work in their small tent in the backyard in the 108-degree heat and installed an earpiece activated by a magnet that gave this young man the privacy he was seeking.

As wonderful as this mission was, it wasn't fulfilling the entire calling that Allen and Drue were looking for and to which they were being drawn.

SimplyHome's technology was groundbreaking, but it could be just out of reach for those who might not be able to afford it, so in 2009, SimplyHome joined with Eblen Charities and created the No Place Like Home program. No Place Like Home helps families by providing the same technology at little or no cost and by refurbishing and repurposing the equipment that might not be used any longer by the person for whom it was created.

Each day tens of thousands of families are served and millions of bits of information are sent to help remove the obstacles that would keep so many people from meeting challenges that most of us could never dream of at home.

It has been said that technology brings us all together by making the world smaller. In some cases that may be true enough, but with Allen and Drue Ray, along with their family and employees at SimplyHome technology, the program opens the world to many by creating possibilities where there once were only limitations.

In his younger years, no matter what he was doing, Allen always asked to be sent where he was needed most.

There is little doubt that Allen and Drue are already there.

Joe, Janice, Allen, and Drue serve as shining examples. In spite of seemingly insurmountable odds and many times walking down a path that darkened at every turn, they refused to be dissuaded as they looked to find their own Calcutta.

Through it all, they persevered when at times there appeared to be no reason at all to keep going. But, as with Mother Teresa, there was "a call within a call," and in following that call, lives were and continue to be made better, each and every day.

Find your own Calcutta.

Let us begin …

Let Us Begin

- Mistakes you may make along the way can help you become who you are meant to be.
- The great things you may do in your life many times begin in small, unexpected places.
- Don't give in to setbacks or what can easily be perceived as failure. They may only be there to better guide you in the right direction.
- Look to connect the dots others are missing. Anyone can connect A to B to C. Rather, look to connect A to R or D to S. By doing so, new worlds of service and possibilities will unfold.
- No matter how long it may take, please do not lose heart. No matter how dark the path may seem, all is not lost. The life of meaning and service you seek is closer than you think.

Chapter 14

A SIMPLE MESSAGE

If I ever become a saint, I will surely be one of
darkness. I will continually be absent from Heaven
to light the light of those in darkness on earth.
—Mother Teresa of Calcutta

In opening an AIDS hospice in our nation's capital in 1986, Mother Teresa spoke on behalf of those she was wishing to serve, saying, "We are not here to sit in judgment on these people, to decide blame or guilt.

"Our mission is to help them, to make their dying days more tolerable. We are not social workers. We may be doing social work, but we are not social workers because we are really trying to be contemplatives right in the heart of the world and because we take Christ at his word. He said, 'You did it to me.' And so we are touching Him twenty-four hours a day."

Mother Teresa's comments were not meant to minimize the wonderful work of those called to serve those in need in their communities through social work. I believe it is just the opposite. She was calling attention to their work but adding that the Missionaries of Charity's work was different; this was to help assuage the great many concerns the surrounding area had in those early days of AIDS, when there were fears of catching the disease through the air or from discarded tissue.

Her comments stated that what she and her sisters proposed was not a government-run program but one that saw those who were suffering, as Mother Teresa would say many times, as "Jesus in distressing disguise."

Each day we have the privilege of working with our local Health and Human Services Department in Buncombe County. I stand in amazement at the unbelievable work that Mandy Stone, Jim Holland, Tracie Franklin, Phillip Hardin, and the others do on behalf of the individuals, children, and families for whom they provide care and services in the midst of crisis.

Their compassion, knowledge, and commitment to our community and those we all serve is second to none and reaches far beyond what is deemed as "social work."

So much of what we do and how we accomplish our outreach is in partnership with them and are our best efforts to emulate their kindness and effectiveness.

They serve those in need as few others I have met. We are fortunate to be part of their outreach; every community should be so fortunate. Their outreach and the selfless service they provide—what they do and how they accomplish it—goes far beyond its being just a job.

As mentioned before, we all must take care that we don't judge the work of others or compare our commitment to others who serve—they may serve in different ways, and that certainly doesn't lessen the impact on the lives they serve. We need to focus on those who call upon us for help and how we can bring them the assistance and care they need.

It doesn't matter what others do. It matters what we do.

Mother Teresa's simple prayer is one that we can keep close to us as a reminder of who our lives of service are for in the first place.

> Deliver me from the desire of being loved.
> From the desire of being extolled.
> From the desire of being honored.
> From the desire of being praised.
> From the desire of being preferred.

From the desire of being consulted.
From the desire of being approved.
From the desire of being popular.
From the fear of being humiliated.
From the fear of being despised.
From the fear of suffering rebukes.
From the fear of being calumniated.
From the fear of being forgotten.
From the fear of being wronged.
From the fear of being ridiculed.
From the fear of being suspected.

Eliminating the desire for praise and the fear of criticism frees us from the insignificant things that hold our hearts captive from reaching our true levels of committing our time, energy, and lives to those in need.

With a free heart and clear vision, we can continue on the path, knowing that the love and care we give to this world will not be hindered by our egos.

In knowing this, we also should know that we are not asked to succeed in everything; we are only asked that we look for those in need and reach out to them with everything we have.

If we are called to reach out and serve others—and who among us is not—we have to continue to do so whether we "feel like it" or not. Far too much is at stake, and far too many are counting on us to help ease their burdens for us to turn our compassion on and off or to withhold our hands because we feel less like helping than we previously did.

Even on our worst days or in the face of our own suffering, we should strive to help make the days of those with whom we come in contact a bit brighter.

In *A Call to Mercy*, one of the sisters of the Missionaries of Charity shared this story:

> I was in the dormitory. It was winter, and all the doors
> and windows were open and I was shivering in my bed.
> Two blankets were not enough, but again it was around

midnight, so I tried to warm myself with what I had. Just then I felt someone covering me with a blanket. I thought I was imagining, yet I opened my eyes and who was there?

Of course, Mother. Once again, very lovingly she covered me, tucked the blankets under my mattress, blessed me, and pressed her warm hands on my face and said, "Sleep."

Only in the morning did I realize that she had sacrificed her own blanket and given it to me. Was she able to sleep in the cold without a blanket? Only Heaven knows. In the morning, Mother told me, "How much the poor have to suffer sleeping on a bare cold floor without any blanket. Our sufferings are nothing compared to the suffering of the poor."

Mother Teresa set a tremendous example for us yet again in the simple act of giving her blanket to one of her sisters. No one knows whether or not Mother Teresa felt like giving up her blanket and being cold herself throughout the night. But that didn't matter; she did it because she knew her sister needed it. She did it because it was who she was.

Would we have done the same? I have heard it said many times, sort of tongue in cheek, "Well, I'm no Mother Teresa ..." But the thing is, Mother Teresa would probably say the same thing. We may not be a Mother Teresa, but she was one of us, and she was the first to admit it.

In her later years, Mother Teresa's health continued to fail, but no matter how ill she felt physically, she continued to set herself aside and help meet the needs of others.

On her last day on earth, Mother Teresa awoke at her regular time, said her morning prayers in her room, and returned to the chapel for mass. Following mass, she went into the hallway to meet with those who came to see her, seeking her help and counsel and to request her prayers; among them was a man and his wife who had just lost their only daughter through suicide. They came seeking understanding of why God had allowed this to happen.

Although not well, Mother Teresa took a great amount of time to talk with them and offered them her prayers and compassion. After she saw everyone who had come to see her, she ate a small breakfast and responded to letters until midday.

After lunch, she joined her sisters for prayer and retired to her room to rest, but she was uneasy as her back ached, and she found sleep unattainable. Unable to rest, Mother Teresa returned to her daily routine of service, attending to the needs of those who came to see her that afternoon and meeting with her sisters.

It wasn't long until fatigue overcame her, and she retired to her room to try to rest. Although her physical pain increased, Mother Teresa, with the help of Sister Nirmala, was able to rest and take some tea and crackers.

When the daily four o'clock chapel service began, Mother Teresa's back was in such intense pain that she was not able to attend, so she lay down on her bed, again without getting much rest.

She did sit up for a short while to receive one of the brothers of the Missionaries of Charity, who was traveling to Singapore that evening and had asked to see her for her blessing and to tell her of his plans. Mother Teresa prayed with him, putting her pain aside, and told him, "I will be with you in spirit always at any place, wherever you may go, assisting you with my prayers."

After he left, she returned to bed, and Sister Nirmala came to be with her and pray together, as they had done almost daily. There was no doubt that she was weakening by the minute. Again, she was left alone to rest, and shortly afterward a call came from Mother Teresa's room: "Sisters, I can't breathe."

They hurried to her door, calling a priest and Mother Teresa's doctor. With her beloved sisters around her, Mother Teresa's last act was to kiss the crucifix that she held and speak her last words, "Jesus, I love you. Thank God, thank God."

Moments later, the lights flickered in the Mother House and went out. They briefly returned, and when they went out the second time the entire city was in darkness, not knowing that the light that had shone so brightly for more than fifty years had gone out, and Mother Teresa was finally home.

Mother Teresa died at 8:30 p.m., and Sister Nirmala confirmed the news to the world an hour later. News of her death spread across the world in a matter of minutes, and messages of condolence came in from every corner of the globe. The government of her adopted country bestowed on her a state funeral usually conveyed for the highest dignitaries of India.

The woman who spent most of her life working in the gutters was, in their eyes, worthy of the highest accolades the nation of India could bestow.

Mother Teresa was laid to rest in a special sepulcher constructed on the first floor of the Mother House.

The white marble marker states simply, "Love one another as I have loved you."

Let us begin …

Let Us Begin

- We must strive to eliminate the desire for praise and the fear of criticism.
- We are not called to succeed. We are called to serve.
- We must be willing to share of what we have, even if it may cause our own discomfort.
- Our focus should not be on what others do or don't do, nor should our focus be on their opinion of what we are called to do. It never matters what they do; it matters what we do.
- Even on the day she died, Mother Teresa continued to see those in need and who sought her council. Her compassion had no limits, and I can't imagine a better example for all of us to follow.

EPILOGUE

Most of us, if we are truly honest with ourselves, have to admit that at one time or another, our lives haven't seemed to make any sense at all.

Every minute of every day, so much is put before us and surrounds us that can easily distract us from what we are called to do. Many times we find ourselves heading down the wrong road or standing there paralyzed, heading down no road at all. We may see the service that is our hearts' desire, and what we see that the world might need is so daunting that we have no idea where to start.

As simple as it may seem, you don't need to know where to start. You don't need a big group, you don't need a committee, and you don't need a consensus. All you need to do is to start.

Remember, Mother Teresa started by picking up just one person. There was no organization behind her, no bank account, and no supporters—just her desire to help the "poorest of the poor."

Cookie Mills, Joe and Janice Brumit, Drue and Allen Ray, and countless others around the world are doing amazing things in their communities by just setting out without any help. They set out, and the help came.

This is something you can do as well. It will be far from easy. You may have to fight a battle more than once to win.

But you will indeed win.

And so will the world.

If you think I might be able to help or offer any additional thoughts, or if you have any stories of those who have found their own Calcutta, I would love to hear and share them. Please feel free to contact me at wmurdock0@icloud.com, or visit www.findyourowncalcutta.com.

Printed in the United States
By Bookmasters